Related Events to the Second Coming of the Christ

THE MILLENNIUM

A Thousand Years of Peace and Prosperity

Volume 7

Michael W. Dewar

Copyright © 2023 by Michael W. Dewar
THE MILLENNIUM: A Thousand Years od Peace and Prosperity
Series: Related Events to the Second Coming of the Christ

ISBN: 979-8-9883484-0-5

Published by Dwelling Place Cleansing
Brooklyn, New York 11236
United States of America
DPSCleansing.com

All rights reserved solely by the author. The author guarantees all contents are original and do not infringe upon the legal rights of any other person or work. No part of this book may be reproduced in any form without the permission of the author.

Unless otherwise indicated, Bible quotations are taken from The Holy Bible, New International Version(NIV). Copyright © 1973, 1978, 1984 by International Bible Society; The Holy Bible, King James Version(KJV); and The Holy Bible, New Living Translation(NLT). Copyright © 1996 by Tyndale House Publishers, Inc.

Dedication

This book is dedicated to honor the memory of Gloria Manning, for her faithful service in the church, support of the pastoral ministry including the contributions of books to the pastor's library. She has long transitioned to be with the Lord, but the pleasing fragrance of her life lived for Christ and neighbors lingers as cherished memories.

THE MILLENNIUM

"Arise O Morning Star, arise and never set!"

CONTENTS

PREFACE vii

INTRODUCTION 9

CHAPTER 1 19

WHAT IS THE MILLENNIUM? 19

CHAPTER 2 27

When Is the Millennium? 27

CHAPTER 3 35

THE PEOPLE OF THE MILLENNIUM 35

CHAPTER 4 45

LIFESTYLE OF THE MILLENNIUM 45

CHAPTER 5 57

THE GOVERNMENT OF THE MILLENNIUM 57

CHAPTER 6 WORSHIP DURING THE MILLENNIUM 71

CHAPTER 7 91

CHARACTER & DURATION OF CHRIST'S REIGN 91

REFERENCE 101

OTHER BOOKS BY THIS AUTHOR 103

ABOURT THE AUTHOR 109

THE MILLENNIUM

PREFACE

In the previous volume (#6) we covered some major end-time events; the primary one is the Armageddon War. Upon His return to earth, Jesus promptly encounters the major gentile world powers united in war against Him with their latest war machines. He puts down all opposing powers to His authority in what is commonly referred to as the War of Armageddon.

The chief opposing actors and emissaries of Satan are the Antichrist, and the False prophet. They lead the attack against Jesus, with a united world behind them. Despite that, they are captured and thrown alive in the lake of burning sulfur (Rev.19:19-20). Their armies and support personnel are killed, and the birds of prey feasted on their dead bodies (v.21).

Satan is taken into custody (Rev.20:1-6). The nations are judge, including Israel, and the judge declares who are given the rite of passage to enter the millennial kingdom (Matt.25:25-46).

The millennium begins the personal and visible reign of Jesus Christ on the earth, sitting on the throne of David (Isa.9:7). This is the literal "thy kingdom of God" that Christians pray about (Matt.6:10 KJV). It God ruling on earth over the kingdoms of men. Handel sums it up in the Messiah, "the kingdoms of the world have become the kingdom of our God and of his Christ."

The millennium answers the questions of peace raised in Lewis Hensley's poem set to music:

> Thy kingdom come, O God,
> thy rule, O Christ, begin;
> break with thine iron rod
> the tyrannies of sin.
>
> Where is thy reign of peace
> and purity and love?
> When shall all hatred cease,
> as in the realms above?
>
> When comes the promised time
> that war shall be no more,
> and lust, oppression, crime
> shall flee thy face before?

In a similar sense, the song of the angels to the shepherds on a Judean hillside at the time of Jesus' birth is also fulfilled in His millennial reign. The angels' song, "Glory to God in the highest heaven, and on earth peace to those on whom his favor rests" (Luke 2:8-14). The millennium will be the first-time earth fully experienced that promise of peace and goodwill.

Let me take this opportunity to, once again, thank those who have helped one way or another to make this and the other volumes in the series possible. And may those who take the time to read them be edified and blessed.

INTRODUCTION
The Perfect Society Envisioned

Humankind has been searching for the perfect society for a long time, the grand Utopia of peace and abundance. Not finding it, they convinced themselves that they are ambitious and intelligent enough to overcome ignorance with science, end wars, economic lack, cure diseases, and bring about the perfect society through education and sheer human ingenuity. They have pushed the boundaries of science to the borders of nuclear extinction, but the perfect society remains elusive.

Yes, we split the atom and invented machines that fly many times faster than the speed of sound. But the perfect society we dreamed of lies in Neverland, comfortably out of our reach.

In fact, World Wars I and II and our stock-pile of nuclear weapons constitute the grim reality that we are closer to destroying ourselves than to our self-achieved perfect society. There is hardly one rational Utopian believer left among the hardened, incurable optimists once lived among us.

History, including Nazi Germany, has taught us that an educated savage may be a little more noble but still a savage. The noble savage has developed new ways to kill his neighbor, not how-to live-in peace, and harmony. His education has made him more dangerous to human survival. Russia's war with Ukraine is, perhaps, the latest example of educated savagery.

Merriam Webster gives us three meanings for Utopia: 1) "a place of ideal perfection, especially in laws, government, and social conditions." 2) "An impractical scheme for social improvement," and 3)"an imaginary and indefinitely remote place."[1] Meaning number one is suitable for our purpose here.

A perfect place, the so-called Utopia, is a concept from Thomas More's fictional work by that name, first published in 1516. The book "depicts a fictional island society and its religious, social, and political customs." It compares social and economic conditions in Europe, at the time, with those of an ideal society on an imaginary island off the coast of the Americas.[2]

As a Greek student myself, I can easily see how More joins two Greek words, "ou" (not, no) and "topas" (place) to form utopia.[3] The word is used today to represent the ideal or the perfect society. In Christian thought or biblical understanding, only the Millennium could equal and supersede More's perfect society. But take note that it is not brought about through *sheer human ingenuity*, as spoken of earlier, the divine is greatly instrumental in the realization of the biblical perfect society.

INTRODUCTION

The True Perfect Society

From a biblical perspective, the true and perfect society is the Kingdom of God on earth. Fundamentally, the Bible is a book about the kingdom of God. It opens with Paradise on earth, but that was short lived as John Milton so aptly illustrates in his classic work, *Paradise Lost*.[4] Because of rebellion against a divine *executive order*, our ancestral parents were driven from paradise, a loss for us all. Humans have been struggling ever since to regain paradise, but only in Jesus Christ is Paradise truly realized, as Milton again observes in *Paradise Regained*.[5]

After the expulsion of humans from Paradise, God sought to establish His kingdom through Israel, a nation He started with the call of Abraham and a promised son named, Isaac (Gen.12:1-9,17:15-22). Through Abraham's grandson, Jacob, the foundation and framework of the nation, Israel, was laid. Jacob's name was later changed to Israel (Gen.32:22-30). Jacob's sons became the twelve tribes of Israel, the nation.

Though a loose confederacy of twelve tribes at first, Israel became a nation under Moses and Joshua, a theocratic kingdom. Israel was united because the people looked back to one father, Abraham. But brothers do fight and at times kill each other, so it was more than kin that held them together. It was the worship of the one God, Yahweh, which was the true cement holding them together. This was the unique quality no other nation of antiquity had, one God. They all had many gods.

But this unique belief in One personal God that served as the glue holding the twelve tribes together as one nation, kept cracking due to idolatry. Idolatry was the experiment of turning from Yahweh to worship other gods. It was Israel's cardinal sin; it held the poison of destroying them as a nation.

Through covenant agreements, Israel pledged to be faithful to Yahweh and be His choice possession, His number one nation on earth, the head and not the tail. God promised to bless, prosper, and give them victory over their enemies (Deut.28:1-14). But if they break covenant and abandon Yahweh to serve other gods, the curse of the covenant would be released, and they would be driven off the land and be scattered to the ends of the earth. They would always be chased by their enemies until they are destroyed or return to God in true repentance (Deut.28:15-68). Idolatry was Israel's perpetual sin and weakness, as the books of Judges to Malachi reveal.

The theocracy fell apart during the time of Samuel. He was the last leader of Israel in that period known as the time of the Judges. This period runs from the death of Joshua to the anointing of the first King by Samuel. During Samuel's tenure, the nation wanted a human king like the surrounding nations.

Distraught over the matter, Samul counseled the nation that God was their King, but they insisted on wanting a king like the other nations around them. Those nations were heathens. God told Samuel that Israel was not deserting Samuel; they were rejecting God ruling over them. God told Samuel to give them what they wanted but be sure to show them the disadvantage of having a human king (1Sam.8:1-21).

Saul was anointed as the first king, and with that Israel transitioned from a theocracy to a monarchy (1 Sam.9: 17-10:1-4). Saul, though having great potentials, was a miserable failure as king over God's people. Eventually, God rejected him and chose David, a man after God's own heart. David was a might warrior, and a great worshiper of Yahweh. He united the nation.

But David was a double-edged sword. On the one hand, he united the nation but on the other, he sowed the seeds of discontent in his family that affected the nation negatively. Like all of us, David was not a perfect man. He was greatly flawed. He committed serious sins that festered into grave family problems that affected the nation. His son Absalom had David on the run. Absalom attempted to overthrow David, seizing the throne to become king by force (2 Sam.15:1-19:8).

There was adultery, murder, incest, rebellion, and the like in David's family. A few of His sons rebelled against him and came close to a successful coupe but they were not God's choice. David's most unlikely son, Solomon, succeeded him.

The nation reached its golden years under David and Solomon. Solomon started out with the favor and wisdom of God, and Israel became the envy among the nations of antiquity. But under Solomon, cracks in the foundation of the nation positioned it for a tectonic shift after his death.

Solomon married foreign women who were daughters of leaders of other nations. These marriages were political; they formed alliances with those nations — that was the upside. The downside was this—these women worshipped their native gods and brought those practices with them. They seduced Solomon from worshipping Yahweh, the God of Israel. Solomon also heavily taxed the people to finance his elaborate projects. His sinful behavior cut short the sustainability of his kingdom.

After Solomon's death, his son Rehoboam came to the throne, but this young man lacked the wisdom of his father and was unable to hold the nation together. He had a half-brother, named Jeroboam, who came out of exile to challenge him for the throne. Jeroboam first asked the young king for some concessions, such as lifting the heavy taxation on the people, among other things. The elders that counseled the king felt that the concessions requested were reasonable and a small price to pay for the unity of the nation (1King 12:1-24).

But the young king refused the counsel of the elders for the counsel of his peers. They advised him to make the burden on his people twice as heavy as that imposed by his father before him. With that arrogance, the nation split into two kingdoms. Ten tribes went to his half-brother, Jeroboam, to form the Northern Kingdom, Israel. He retained two tribes (Judah, and Benjamin) as the Southern kingdom, Judah (2 Kings 12:1-24).

The Northern Kingdom under Jeroboam was most wicked, and in the process of time they were overrun and taken captives into exile to Assyria. They disappeared from the face of the earth and are referred to as the *Ten Loss Tribes*.

The other two tribes that formed the Kingdom of Judah, or the Southern Kingdom succumbed to Idolatry and were taken exile to Babylon (Jer.39-40). After seventy years a remnant returned from Babylon and Persia to rebuild the temple and the wall of Jerusalem. But the nation has never regained the luster it had under David and Solomon. But God promised to regather them from among the nations He scattered them.

By the time of Jesus, the Romans occupied Israel. They had a new temple much larger than Solomon's temple and the rebuilt Zerubbabel's Temple (Ezra 1-3). The Jewish religion was flourishing, but they longed for the nation to be restored to independence and its former glory. They knew God would send a Messiah, a leader like king David to throw off the Roman yoke. Periodically, a false Messiah, a political revolutionary like Barabbas would emerge but only to be crushed by the Romans.

Eventually, Israel became weary of anyone claiming to be Messiah. Israel leaders under Rome enjoyed a decent living by accommodation and were afraid of losing that by embracing false Messiahs. They became so guarded that they rejected the true Messiah when He arrived in the person of Jesus of Nazareth. If Jesus were willing to be king on the terms of Caiaphas and his cronies, they would have accepted Him.

But Jesus could not accept the terms of the backslidden, religious elite of Judaism, without foregoing His plan of redemption. The religious elite did not understand Messiah to be the Son of God, such claim was blasphemous to them. As corrupted as Judaism was, they were not going to make that compromise. Neither could Jesus compromise His position, so they rejected Him and conspired to kill Him. They succeeded having Him crucified by manipulating Pilate (John 19:12).

The Kingdom Postponed

Old Testament prophets, directly or indirectly, prophesied the coming of the Kingdom and they did so in the context of the coming of the Messiah (Isa.9: 6-7; Dan.2: 44).

As in Daniel, the Kingdom of God is often viewed in the context of kingdoms headed by humans. In some passages it destroys and replaces the kingdoms of men. Handel in the Messiah sums it this way, "the kingdoms of this world have become the Kingdom of God and of His Christ."

During the time of Jesus' ministry on earth, Israel's leaders were looking for a literal political kingdom, as glorious as that ruled over by David and Solomon. For that reason, the disciples kept asking Jesus, at what time He would restore the kingdom to Israel? But Jesus kept talking about a kingdom utterly different from the one they had in mind. Jesus speaks of an invisible spiritual kingdom. "The kingdom of God is among you" or "the kingdom of God is in you" or the kingdom of heaven is at hand or "pray thy kingdom come" are terms used by Jesus. But what did He really mean by such expressions?

Jesus meant that the spiritual aspect of the kingdom of God or of heaven precedes the visible, material manifestation of the God's kingdom of earth. Why? God wanted to first establish His rule in the hearts of humans, to empower them to rule or govern a literal kingdom in righteousness, peace, and justice.

Without that inner, spiritual transformation, humans have the deep-seated propensity to plunge a thousand "Paradises" into the jangling discord of a corrupt, war ridden ghetto. By nature, we human are deprave; we want to go our own way (Isa.53:6; Rom.1:18-32). Israel's history is one of backsliding, going their own way and destroying a goodly, earthly kingdom.

God must first establish spiritual rule in their hearts to qualify them to keep an earthly kingdom reflecting the glory of God. It is on this level Israel kept resisting God in constant backsliding and idolatry. The written law on tables of stone was powerless to restrain them (Rom.8:2-3).

Israel rejected the Messiah; they refused to be won inwardly. They refused the spiritual rule of God in their hearts. As a result, the Church was established to bring about the spiritual rule of God in the hearts of humankind worldwide (John 3:16-17; Matt.28:19-20; Acts 2:22-39).

Because of their unbelief, God could not use Israel for this phase of His kingdom program. He put them aside, postponing the realization of the kingdom they so desperately wanted. Of course, this putting aside of Israel was not meant to be permanent (Rom.9-11). At the time appointed, God will make good on all the covenantal promises made to Israel.

Despite their unfaithfulness toward God, Israel remains God's covenant people. They might be trucebreakers, but God is the covenant-maker and the promise keeper. All the covenant promises made to Israel will be fulfilled in the future millennial kingdom. But those promises cannot be realized until Israel as a nation embraced Jesus of Nazareth as the true Messiah. That will happen, indeed! Zechariah (12:10) gives up the following prophetic, intelligence report:

> And I will pour out on the house of David and the inhabitants of Jerusalem a spirit of grace and supplication. They will look on me, the one they have pierced, and they will mourn for him as one mourns for an only child, and grieve bitterly for him as one grieves for a firstborn son. (Zech.12:10)

This will happen when Jesus returns from heaven to rescue Israel from annihilation by the Antichrist, a false messiah Israel's leader signed a treaty with at the onset of the Great Tribulation (see Vol.3, *The Great Tribulation Survival Guide*...).

After the Judgment of nations (including Israel), the millennial kingdom will begin. It is during this time all the covenant promises to Israel will be fulfilled through Jesus Christ, Israel's true Messiah and reigning King over all the earth.

THE MILLENNIUM

CHAPTER 1

WHAT IS THE MILLENNIUM?

The Reality of the Millennium

The word "millennium" is commonly used now a days; we even named one generation, *millennials.* Yet, most people do not know what the word means and where it comes from. It is fundamentally a Bible word, used in the Church for many centuries now. It comes from two Lattin words, *mille,* which means, a thousand, and *annus* which means, year.[1] Millennium, therefore, is one thousand years, and points to the future reign of Christ over the earth in fulfillment of prophecy.

The Bible speaks of this thousand-year period six times in one chapter alone (Rev.20:1-8). For most of us Bible scholars, it is no fiction! The millennium is most significant, it fulfills that line in the Lord's Prayer that says, "thy kingdom come, thy will be done one earth as it is in heaven" (Matt.6: 9-10 KJV). That quality of life can only be achieved when Christ Himself is at the controls of world government as reigning KING of Kings and LORD of Lords (Rev.19:11-15). It is the time Satan is bound and removed to prison (Rev.20:1-3).

Other Millennium Scriptures

The millennium is frequently spoken of in both Old and New Testaments, not in terms of number of years, but in the context of the kingdom of God or the reign of God or the restoration of the kingdom to Israel. The period is referred to as a time of peace and unprecedented prosperity (Isa.32:1-8, 16-20).

The conditions for Israel and all the people of God will be most glorious during the millennial age. Through the Abrahamic covenant, God promised to bless the whole world through the Messiah (Gen.12:1-3). For this reason, Israel is often used to describe the conditions of the whole earth under the Messiah (Isa.35:1-10). Bible scholars sometimes make the mistake, limiting the blessings under the Messiah to Israel. While Israel's position in God's program is pivotal, it is also clear that Israel is used as a conduit nation for the blessing of all nations upon the earth. Note the clause in the promise to Abraham, "... and all peoples on earth will be blessed through him" (Gen.12:3).

During the millennium, God's covenantal promises to Israel will be fully realized because it will be the first time Israel as a nation fully embrace Jesus of Nazareth as their Messiah. By extension the whole earth will be as God envisions it to be. Had our ancestral parents not sinned, handing-off the governance of the earth to Satan, placing it under God's curse, full blessing would have been realized before the millennium (Gen.3:17-19; Rom.8:18-25). Or perhaps, a millennium would be unnecessary.

There is another way to look at it—because Israel was set aside, God has blessed the whole world through the Church that was raised up to do the work Israel disqualified herself to do by rejecting the Messiah (John 1:12). So then, Israel that should have been first to be blessed becomes the last to get the fulness of God's blessings. Whatever way we may look at it, the Millennial kingdom will be a unique and exceptional time.

The Millennium marks the end of Satan's reign over the earth; his tenancy has ended, and the true Landlord has taken over His property; He alone has the title deed (Ps. 24:1). Satan is evicted, forcibly bound, removed, and in custody (Rev.20:1-3). The millennium is what the earth could have been, had our ancestral parents not trusted Satan in the paradise garden.

During His first advent, Jesus wept openly over Jerusalem due to their unbelief (Matt.23:37-39). The raising of His friend, Lazarus, is another example of Jesus weeping publicly. The raising of Lazarus accompanied with public weeping were not done exclusively out of sympathy for or to benefit Mary and Martha but for the whole nation, to turn Israel from their unbelief toward the Messiah (John 11:35-53). A handful of Jews did believe, but despite this dramatic miracle, the nation became more intransigent in their rejection of Jesus (vv.45-53).

Because of Israel's wholesale rejection of the Messiah, the spiritual blessings of Isaiah 40 and many other Old Testament prophecies could not be realized in the nation at the time of Jesus' first advent. But they will be fulfilled during the millennial period when David's Son sits upon his throne and rules in righteousness and justice as prophesied (Isa.9: 6-7). God's word will not fall to the ground but will come to pass at the proper time as determined by God (Isa.55:8-11).

The Humanist's Utopia

For a long time, humankind has been searching for the perfect society, one free from war, disease, and lack. They thought that through education and human ingenuity, they could bring about the perfect, Utopian society. But with the advent of World War, I and II that dream has largely evaporated.

Of course, there are a few who still believe the beast can be tamed to build a better society. Others have concluded that humans without God are nothing short of an educated savage, speeding toward his own self-destruction.

There are those among us who believe that humankind is exactly what the Word of God diagnosed his condition to be, deprave, sinful, and even reprobate (Rom.1:18-32). Humans have a spiritual disease that alienates them from God and neighbor. Jeremiah speaks of the human inner sanctum as deprave, deceitful and desperately wicked, beyond self-understanding. Only God Himself understands the full depravity of the human condition (Jer.17: 9-10).

Humankind needs a redeemer, one who can cure him of his spiritual malady. The good news is, God has provided such a person; His name is Jesus Christ (John 3:14-17). The angel Gabriel informs Joseph and Mary that this Jesus will save His people from their sins (Matt.1:21; Luke1:29-31). But when Messiah came, His own people rejected Him (John 19:1-16).

Despite His own people's rejection, Jesus still laid down His life for the redemption of humankind, some embraced Him as Savior and Lord, while most humans continue in their lost, deprave lifestyle. Now, Jesus has returned to put down all opposition to His authority and to reign as Savior, Lord, and King over the earth. Here, humans are given another chance to be redeemed as He Jesus establishes the near perfect society.

Restoration of the Davidic Kingdom

The millennium is at least the restoration of the Davidic kingdom to Israel. Throughout the earthly ministry of the Lord Jesus, His disciples kept asking for the kingdom to be restored to Israel or at least, to tell them when. But Jesus returned to heaven without that request being answered, except that the Father by His own authority sets the time of restoration (Acts 1:6-7).The implication of this answer is that the kingdom will not be restored until some future date, evidently, during the Lord's *Second Advent.* That date is classified.

But not that highly classified. We already know if the kingdom were not restored during Christ's *First Advent*, it must be done during His *Second Advent*. There are many covenant-related promises to Israel and the Church that are yet to be fulfilled, and they all point to the Messiah's second coming.

The golden years of Israel's History were under king David and Solomon. God made David a promise that a son of his linage will always sit on his throne. We know that Son is Jesus, the Messiah, whom Israel rejected and continues to reject for two thousand years of Church history. At any time since the crucifixion of Jesus, Jews could have reexamined the record of Jesus of Nazareth and change their position about His authenticity but instead, they remained stuck in unbelief.

The restoration of the Davidic Kingdom will not just benefit Israel but all the nations on earth that will be allowed to enter the millennial reign of the Christ. The millennial kingdom is the kingdom of God upon the earth, it is the combination of exercising rule over the natural domain as well as the spiritual. The kingdoms of this world will become "the Kingdom of our God and of His Christ" as Handel reminds us in the Messiah.

The first advent of the Christ was primarily intended to redemptively establish the spiritual kingdom, the rule of God in the hearts of humankind through Israel. But Israel failed at that because they rejected the Messiah. For that reason, the Church was established and given that assignment to win the hearts of mankind through the good news of the gospel of salvation.

Humans must first be won inwardly; they cannot build a perfect society without inner spiritual transformation (John 3:1-21; Rom.12:1-2). National Israel rejected the Messiah, and in doing so, they rejected the redemption plan of God. God set them aside and established the Church to carry out His plan of redemption. The plan is to establish His rule in the inner sanctum of humankind. This is what Jesus meant when He said, "the kingdom of God is in you" (Luke 17:21 KJV).

Israel was temporarily set aside because of spiritual blindness, unbelief. But God has not cast away or abandoned His covenant people. Blindness happened in part to Israel until the fulness of the gentiles is brought into God's the kingdom, then Israel's blindness will be lifted to recognize Yeshua as their true Messiah. With that recognition all Israel will be saved, as Saint Paul discussed (Rom.9-11).

Though national Israel remains in unbelief today, God is still at work in the restoration of the modern State of Israel, and in the regathering of Jews to their covenant land. This regathering is called, *Zionism*.[2] The regathering and restoration will continue through the Great Tribulation when God seals 144,000 Jewish evangelists to preach the gospel to Israel and Jews globally to prepare them to receive Yeshua as their Messiah upon His return the second time (Rev.7:1-17).

The regathering of Israel to their covenant land will be completed upon the return of the Messiah when all Israel will be saved. That means, they must be won inwardly first; the rule of God must be established in their hearts. No Jew or Gentile who rejects Jesus Christ will be allowed to enter the kingdom.

To emphasize, Israel can only be saved by acknowledging and receiving Jesus as their true Messiah (John 3:14-21). No human being will have the luxury of bypassing Jesus Christ and be saved. Every knee must bow, and every tongue must confess of His Lordship to the glory of God the Father (Philip.2:9-11). The gift of salvation from sin and eternal life are resident in the person of Jesus Christ alone (John 3:16; Acts 4:12).

Until then, some Jews will come to faith and salvation during the Church age by embracing Jesus as their Messiah, Savior, and Lord; we call them messianic Jews. We should not forget that the Church started predominantly with Jews.

Unbelieving Jews and Gentiles will continue to strive for the illusive perfect society through education, technological advancement, and even religion. But only the Almighty God through His Son, Jesus Christ, can bring about that perfect society. For that reason, He instructed us to pray, "[Let] your kingdom come, your will be done, on earth as it is in heaven" (Matt.6:9-10). The Millennium is the fulfillment of these two petitions in the Lord's Prayer.

Summary

What is the Millennium? It is not the humanist's perfect society or Utopia, brought about through the depraved genius of humankind. Imperfect humanity cannot build a perfect society. Fallen humans need the help of God to redemptively transform them from within because their problem is fundamentally a spiritual one.

The millennium is the literal rule or reign of Jesus Christ on and over this earth; it is the kingdom of God on earth. It is Christ sitting on the throne of David in Jerusalem as the head of a global theocratic government (Isa.9:7).

With the *Second Advent* of the Christ, the times of the Gentiles come to its end; all Gentile powers terminate. The millennium begins Kingdom Age. Israel will be given rule through the Messiah because certain promises made under the Abrahamic and Davidic covenants will now be fulfilled. The previously rejected Messiah now sits on the throne of David, ruling over the earth.

But Jesus is not just a Jewish Messiah but the Messiah, KING of Kings and LORD of Lords over all the earth and all humankind. The millennium is a time of unprecedented peace and prosperity, such as earth has not seen since the debacle in the paradise garden with our ancestral parents.

CHAPTER 2

WHEN IS THE MILLENNIUM?

Simply stated, the Millennium is Christ ruling upon and over the earth as the head of government for a thousand years; it will be a time of unprecedented peace and prosperity. There will be no wars, no disease, no lack, no devil; life with be perfect in a near perfect society (Rev.20:1-10).

Later in this book, a more prescriptive view of that period will be given, but for now this is essentially what the millennium will be, a near perfect society under Jesus Christ as its King. Later, you will see why it is "near perfect" and not "perfect."

Three Millennium Views

The study of the millennium falls under the branch of theology known as eschatology, which means, *the study of the last things*. Like everything else, all Christian faith traditions do not agree on the millennium. In fact, there are three distinct views or schools of thought concerning the millennium: the pre-millennial view, the amillennial, and the post-millennial views.

Postmillennialism, as it is generally called, is the theological perspective that what Scripture refers to as the perfect society of peace and prosperity, will be brought about by education and the progressive ingenuity of humankind during the Church age. The perfect society will come to fruition between the first and second advent the Christ. There will be no thousand-year reign of a divine being over the earth. There will be no literal thousand-year reign of Christ. Christ will return indeed, the wicked will be judged, and the eternal state will be established.

How did they come to this conclusion? The short answer is, they adhere to a method of scriptural interpretation called *spiritualization.* This method of interpretation is clearly subjective; Scripture means anything the interpreter says it means, so everybody can decide his or her own convoluted meanings and impose them upon the text of Scripture.

The more accurate method of interpretation is the literal method. With this approach, Scripture means exactly what it says, unless it is clearly nonsensical to take it at face value. The literal method of interpretation abides by the historical, grammatical, syntactical, and contextual meaning of words; it abides by the notion that Scripture interprets Scripture. The meaning evolves out of the text, not imposed upon the text.

Again, the literal method of scriptural interpretation refrains from the reader reading his or her opinion into the text, a behavior commonly referred to as *eisegeting.* With the literal method, the interpreter does the very opposite; it is called *exegeting.* The reader pulls out the meaning from the text, not imposing his or her opinion upon the text.

Postmillennialism not only ascribes to humans the power to bring about the perfect society, but it also sees all the covenant promises made to Israel as being fulfilled in the Church. The Church, therefore, replaces Israel. This is an erroneous and greatly flawed understanding of Scripture. Israel in the postmillennial scheme of things would be a cast away nation and people. Scripture clearly teaches the opposite.

During the Church age (from the resurrection of the Christ to His Second Advent), Israel is set aside, temporarily, until the fulness of the gentiles are brought into the God's kingdom. Israel continues to play a pivotal role in God's program, a fact the apostle Paul made clear in his epistle to the Romans and the apostle John in Revelation (Rom.9-11). Revelation (7:1-17) clearly shows God turning His focus on Israel again. Jesus returns in the nick of time to rescue Israel from being annihilated by gentile powers, led by the Antichrist (19:11-21).

World War I and II clearly demonstrate to the world that humans by their own ingenuity will not bring about a perfect society; left to themselves, humans will self-destruct. With that revelation, postmillennialism died under its own weight. No scholar of significance advocates that view today. Most of the postmillennial advocates moved to the amillennialism camp.

Amillennialism. This camp holds the belief that there will not be a millennium, in terms of Christ literally reigning on and ruling over the earth for a thousand years as the head of government. Their beliefs are closely aligned with the now defunct postmillennialism view, except they don't believe mankind by his own genius will bring about the perfect society. God is doing that through His Church. To them, Christ is reigning and ruling over the earth from heaven through the Church now.

This is a view influenced by Saint Augustin's understanding of history, his theology, and the role of the Church. To him all humankind belong to one of two cities by predestination: the City of God or the Secular City.[1] Some have mistakenly made the city of God identical with the Church; thus, the millennium is Christ rule over the Church. So, the scripture verses about the kingdom are fulfilled in the Church.

The problem is, the Church has suffered violence since its birth on the Day of Pentecost. When it controlled government under Constantine, it became corrupted and violent so it could not be identical to the kingdom of God. Because of Augustine's influence this mistaken view is widely held among Catholics and some protestants but is erroneous as the postmillennial view.[2]

Again, amillennialists believe scripture passages that speak of the literal rule of Christ upon and over the earth are fulfilled in the Church; they signify Christ's rule from heaven over His Church. This view is popular the Western Church and among reformed theologians, but it distorts the Scriptures.[3]

Premillennialism is the dominant view today among several Protestant groups or faith traditions; it has the weight of biblical scholarship on its side. It relies on the literal method of biblical interpretation. This group is not a monolith, all believers do not agree exactly. For example, there are those who believe that righteous persons of both the Old and New Testaments will be resurrected at the same time. While others believe in a separate resurrection for each group: one for the church and the other for Israel. Those that view a separate resurrection for Israel tend to be rigidly dispensational in their theology. Once they commit to that system, they stay with it.

The one resurrection group holds to the view that Christ will call for His people of both old and new covenants at once, and they are moved to heaven. This way, the righteous living are safe from the wrath of the Lamb. This event is the rapture (1Thess.4:16-18). It is discussed in volume 1 of this series.

In heaven the people will be safe from the wrath of the Lamb which is poured out upon unbelievers and the resources of the earth that make life comfortable for them. This time of wrath is commonly referred to as the *Great Tribulation* period.

Premillennialists teach that God has a special role for Israel, because the Church has not fully replaced Israel in God's program. God is faithful and will fulfill all His covenant promises made to Israel. The apostle Paul speaks of this role at length in His Epistle to the Romans, chapters 9 to 11.

Christ will return to earth to end the Great Tribulation; He is accompanied with a massive army of saints and angels. He comes to put down all oppositions to His authority, to establish His kingdom, and reign on and over the earth for a thousand years (Rev.19:11-20:1-15). This is the period referred to as the Millennium. This is the position of this author and study series.

The Millennium Begins

The *Millennial Kingdom* is established upon the earth after the return of Christ to earth and following a series of major events.

First, it is important to remember that the *Great Tribulation* is seven years in duration, as discussed in volume 3 (*The Great Tribulation Survival Guide...*). Christ returns to earth with His people (as shown in Vol.5) to end the *Great Tribulation* period.

Second, He overthrows and removes the government of earth, headed by the Antichrist and the False prophet in the Armageddon War. This brings an end the rule of gentile powers.

Third, there will be the judgment of nations including Israel, as well as a massive postwar cleanup, among other events (see

Volume 6). The millennial kingdom under the reign of the Christ is established after these events.

Two Necessary Antecedence

By necessary antecedence, I mean certain indispensable events that must take place before the millennial kingdom of Christ rule is established upon the earth. In this section I will name two such events: 1) the full ingathering of Jews from among the nations to their covenant land, and 2) a Jewish State in place.

The Old Testament is fraught with end-time prophecies of God regathering His people from among the nations of the earth to resettle them in their covenant land (Deut.30:1-6). Moses, speaking by the Holy Spirit knew Israel would not keep faith, that the curse of the covenant would be released, dispersing them to the ends of the earth. But God in His faithfulness would bring them back to their covenant land in keeping with His purpose.

The prophets Ezekiel (20:37-38, 37:1-14) and Daniel(7:18-17) who prophesied during the Babylonian captivity speak comprehensively to include not only of a regathering in their time but of the end-time regathering of all Israel as well.

For two thousand years, Israel has been driven off their covenant land and scattered among the gentile powers of the earth. At the turn of the Twentieth Century, we began to see another Exodus out from among the nation of the earth back to Palestine.[4] We witnessed the miraculous rebirth of the modern Jewish State in 1948, nothing short of divine intervention.

This ingathering and regathering of Israelites will be completed with the second coming of the Christ. He will do the final identification as to who are the true covenant people or descendants of Abraham. There are many who are Jews and do not know it and perhaps there are those who say they are Jews and are not (Rev.2:9). The Messiah will do the final separation.

The bottom line is this, for the Messiah to sit on the throne of King David and rule over the earth from Jerusalem, there must be a fully functional Jewish State upon His arrival. The fact that the Jewish State is already in place, signals the closeness of His coming and the establishment of the Millennial Kingdom.

Israel's Unique Role

Throughout this book, it has been made evident that Israel has a pivotal role to play among nations and in God scheme of things. Yet, a person would be uninformed to say, Jews received preferred treatment, as some are quick to say. Knowing the suffering of Jewish people throughout history, it is hard to conclude that such horrors constitute preferred treatment.

The fact is, God gave them certain principles that work for any people group that put them in practice. Like anyone else, to receive eternal life, one must embrace Jesus the Messiah, as Savior and Lord. All Israel will embrace Yeshua as their Messiah. There is no exception whether you be Jews or Gentiles. If you are outside of Christ, you are lost, because apart from Jesus Christ there is no salvation (John 3:16; Acts 4:12).

Summary

The Millennial Kingdom is the literal rule of Jesus Christ, Son of God, Son of Man, upon and over the earth as KING of kings and LORD of lords after He returns to this earth. The kingdom will be established after the War of Armageddon and the Judgment of Nations (JN). The JN determine who is given the rite of passage to enter the millennial Kingdom of the Christ (Matt. 25:31-46). There are those who will reign with Christ.

The State of Israel will play a pivotal role. For that reason, Christ returns to rescue Israel from annihilation by the Antichrist forces, and to sit on the throne of David and rule over the earth from Jerusalem in righteousness and justice (Isa. 9:6-7). During the Messiah's reign, all the covenant promises made to Israel will be fulfilled.

The Millennium also serves as the restoration of the Kingdom to Israel. This is the question the disciples frequently asked Jesus, when will you restore the kingdom to Israel? They asked it again shortly before His ascension, "Lord, will you at this time restore the kingdom to Israel?" (Acts 1: 6). Jesus replied, "It is not for you to know the times and dates the Father has set by his own authority," he said (v.7). The matter is classified.

The millennial kingdom will be one thousand years of peace and unprecedented prosperity upon the earth, such as never before seen since the fall of humankind in the *Paradise Garden*.

It is the conclusion of this study, that the Premillennial perspective is the accurate view because it is based upon the literal interpretation of Scripture. The literal method puts allegories and all other figures of speech in their rightful place.

The spiritualization method of interpretation is dangerous because it projects the reader's opinion into the text, in which case, every reader can give the text his or her own meaning. But the literal method allows the text to speak for itself. This approach carries the weight of scholarly community, and it leaves little or no room for reader's subjective views.

When will the Millennium begin? It begins sometime after Christ returns with the righteous from heaven to end the Great Tribulation.

CHAPTER 3

THE PEOPLE OF THE MILLENNIUM

A Selective Population

Only righteous people and nations will be allowed to enter the *Millennial Kingdom* of the Christ. In other words, a person's relationship with Jesus Christ in word and deeds is the only measure of righteousness by which entrance is granted to the millennial kingdom. These will fall in several large groups.

First, the large group that returns from heaven with the Christ to end the *Great Tribulation* (Rev.19:11-15). This group includes following three sub-groups:

1) The resurrected righteous dead of both Old and New Testament eras that were taken to heaven in the

Rapture (Dan.12:13; 1Thess. 4:16-18). J.D. Pentecost postulates that OT saints will not be resurrected with the church. They will be resurrected when Christ returns at the end of the Great Tribulation.[1] This writer takes exception to that position. Jesus indicates there will be one-fold and one shepherd (John 10:14-16).

2) The group of living saints, transformed and taken to heaven at the rapture (1Thess.4:16-18; 1Cor.15:50-56).

3) The resurrected saints of the *Great Tribulation* period, those raptured to heaven, perhaps, in two groups (Rev.7: 9-17, 15: 1-4).

Second, resurrected martyrs of the latter part of the *Great Tribulation* period (Rev.20: 4-5), and survivors without the mark of the beast because they were in hiding (Rev.15:1-4). Christ will judge these two groups. Those that took a public stand, resisting and refusing the mark of the beast or worshiping his image and were slaughtered. Those killed early in the tribulation are honored with resurrection to join their brethren in heaven. But those killed much later are resurrected upon Christ return to earth; they enter the kingdom with Him.

Human beings are very resilient; they will go through extraordinary means to live. They will hide out in mountains and caves across the world until the Antichrist's regime runs out the clock and Jesus returns (Rev.19:11-21). So, there will be people who survived the *Great Tribulation* without taking the mark of the beast. They will say yes to Christ and be given the rite of passage to enter His Millennial Kingdom with Christ.

Third, Israel as a nation will enter the millennium. Nations are made up of individuals and families. Israel as a nation will embrace Jesus as their long looked for Messiah. Their spiritual blindness will be lifted to recognize and embrace the Messiah. But let it be made clear, Jews who accepted the mark of the *beast during the Great Tribulation are eternally lost as* gentiles that did the same. It is our relationship with Jesus Christ that makes the difference, whether we be Jew or gentile.

The Jews of national Israel will have three advantages during the *Great Tribulation period.* (1) Because of Israel's treaty with the Antichrist (Dan.9:27), they will not be required to take the mark of the beast until the treaty is broken which is in the second half of the seven-year tribulation when all are forced to worship the beast without exception (Rev.13:14-16). (2) The special ministry of the 144, 000 Jewish evangelist sealed to preach the gospel to the Jews. (3)The rescue of Israel from annihilation by the appearance of the Messiah (see Vol.6).

Fourth, certain Gentile nations will enter the millennial kingdom. The Bible refers to them as sheep nations; they apparently have a supportive posture toward Israel and Christians (Matt.25:31-46). They must have had the firepower to resist the Antichrist regime but not powerful enough to defeat or unnecessarily confront it in open warfare. The Antichrist regime may have decided not to squander limited resources fighting them since they were no hindrance achieving their military objectives. The antichrist regime ran out of time.

These sheep nations will be given rite of passage to enter the Millennium with their identity intact. But on what basis? The simple answer is, based on their relationship with Jesus Christ. Because of its complexity, this needs a little unpacking.

A nation can have just or unjust foreign policy toward other nations. One U.S. administration refers to certain countries in terms not polite to mention here. Foreign policy can be preferential and discriminatory. Therefore, the active, official policy of a nation will reflect if that nation measures up to that level of righteousness God requires to enter the millennial kingdom of the Christ.

For example, if a nation's official policy is to exterminate the Jews, destroys the Jewish State, and occupy their covenant land, as the Antichrist's coalition of nations wanted to do to Israel, we know that is not righteous. It is a clear indication that these nations fail to meet the required criteria to enter the Millennial Kingdom of the Christ. They will not survive, as we will see later in this chapter.

Furthermore, persons who received the mark of the beast during the *Great Tribulation* period will not be allowed to enter the millennial reign of the Christ (Rev.13:8). Why? Because this group pledged allegiance to Satan and were sealed by the mark of the beast as Satan's property (vv.15-18). God also seals His people(Eph.1:13-14; Rev.7:1-8).

Those persons with the mark of the beast were in line with the regime of the Antichrist; they were free from persecution and coercion to live life more comfortably. Only people with the mark of the beast have access to resources. They could earn their keep, buy, and sell, go, and come at liberty because they have the required government credentials or ID to do so.

Those who refused the mark of the beast credentials have only one valid reason for refusal; they have loyalty to Jesus Christ or the God of the Bible. Such persons are hunted down and killed when found. This program is global, and so is the resistance. Millions will be discovered and killed but millions will survive as well. Now Christ makes the determination who is given rite of passage to the millennial kingdom.

The Word of God is clear that people who receive the mark of the beast are lost; their eternal dwelling is with their lord Satan whom they served. These are children of perdition and will not enter the millennial reign of the Christ. By their own choice they gave their allegiance to Satan. It is only right that they share Satan's destiny in the lake of burning sulfur with the beast and the false prophet (Rev.19:19-21, 20: 10).

Millennium Selection Process

The Judgment of Nations is the chief selection process to determine rite of passage to the millennial kingdom. Not all nations will be destroyed, some will retain their identity and be allowed to enter the millennial kingdom of the Christ. But again, the basis on which they are allowed to enter the millennial kingdom is their relationship with Jesus Christ and His covenant people Israel (Matt.25:31-46).

There are two covenant peoples: *Jews and Christians*, Old and New Testament peoples. The Old Testament (OT) is largely Israelites, and the New is largely Gentiles. Note, I did not say, "exclusively," I said, "largely." The OT people of God is a mixed multitude. The same is true with the NT people of God.

The two most important commandments are love for God and love for neighbor. Jesus made it clear in His Sermon on the Mount and throughout the gospels that love for God and neighbor are inextricable bound together (Matt.5:43-48).

If you love God, it will be manifested in compassionate deeds to neighbors. The love for neighbor mandate is where most religious people fail in their duty to God (Matt.22:34-40; Luke 10:25-37;1John 3:10-18). Again, Jesus said, "Blessed are the merciful for they shall obtain mercy" (5:7), and "Blessed are the peacemakers for they shall be called the children of God" (5:9). Love is not warmongering, not holocaust seeking, or genocide embracing. The God of the Bible calls us to do "justly and love mercy" and to walk in humility before Him (Micah 6:8).

For these reasons among others, there will be many surprises in this selection process for the millennial kingdom. People and nations who think they will be chosen may very well be rejected and people and nations who thought they will not stand a chance, may be equally surprised, they are chosen. The surprises are seen in Matthew (25:34-40).

The official policy of a nation toward Israel appears to be significant in this determination as to what nation enters the millennium with its identity. The Judgment of Nations divides the nations into two separate camps: sheep and goats. Only the sheep nations are given rite of passage to enter the millennial kingdom of the Christ. Again, entrance is based upon their relationship with Christ and how they treat people, especially the people of God, including Israel (Matt.25:31-33, 40-46).

Diverse Population

God loves diversity. Diversity is evident at all levels of creation. The human family bears the image and likeness of God, and like the Godhead, it has unity and diversity. The Millennial Kingdom of the Christ will have angels of various ranks, and humans of varying ranks as well, each has its own unique purpose.

Undoubtedly, angels will continue in their current function. They are in the company that returns to earth with the Christ (Rev.19:14). They are powerful beings in the service of God's kingdom; they are intelligent, organized and disciplined.

Humans will fall into two main categories: glorified and unglorified persons. Glorified persons are those that were resurrected or transformed; most went to heaven and returned from heaven with Christ. This group also includes those that Jesus raised from the dead upon His return to earth.

These glorified people are not angels, but they are like angels to some degree. For example, like angels, they will not be married and engaged in human reproduction (Matt.22:28-30; Luke 20:34-36). This will be a vast population of Old and New Testament saints.

Unglorified human beings are both Jews and Gentiles who have not experienced death or transformation from mortal to immortality and are given rite of passage to enter the millennium. They will continue family life as usual, marrying, raising children, and populating the earth. Millions will be born during the millennium, several generations, in fact.

Work and Family Life

The Bible opens with God at work, and it ends with God at work, creating a new heaven and a new earth. God gave man his first job and later told him that by the sweat of his face he would eat bread (Gen.2:15, 3:17-19). Better stated, he must earn his keep.

The Fall of humankind turned work into toil, and hard labor. Hard labor is a curse, not work; work is a blessing. With the curse removed from creation at the second coming of Christ, toil and hard labor will be gone and pleasure returns to work again (Rom.8:22-27). The earth will be more fruitful and productive, not needing the excess human toil to give its return. People won't live to work, so they will enjoy life much better.

Most of the fears of life, the negatives that we now face on earth, will be forever gone during the millennium. The earth will have its Edenic blessings restored. Children will be safe; aging will not be as debilitating, and death will not be scarry. Yes, the unglorified people will still die, for death is not yet destroyed. It is the last enemy that will be destroyed (I Cor.15:26).

Life and work, marriage, and family building, will go on as they do today, but with much more ease and delight for sure. Remember, our archenemy, Satan, will be in prison, chronically wicked people will not be as prevalent as they are today.

Rebels in the Millennium

The Millennium, however, will not be without problems. But compared to the societies we now enjoy or endure worldwide, the Millennium will be paradise perfect, almost. But how come we will still have rebels? You could ask the same question about heaven. It was and is a perfect place, but we read, "Then war broke out in heaven, Michael and his angels fought against the dragon, and his angels fought back" (Rev.12:7).

At the time of Lucifer's rebellion, the blessed Holy Trinity resided in heaven as today. But right there in heaven the first rebel started an uprising. Of course, it was quickly put down and the rebel expelled (vv. 8-9). But how could that happen? It certainly leaves you thinking and asking, "where in heavens did Lucifer get this hellish, evil idea?" That is the million-dollar question we mortals have not been able to answer, yet.

During the millennium, Jesus will be literally reigning on earth with the righteous. Satan will be in prison, so people can hardly say, *the devil made me do it*. How then do we account for rebels? Put your thinking cap on and let's solve it together.

Satan is in prison through the full length of the millennium, so you cannot blame him (Rev.20:1-3). All the people that entered the millennium are righteous people, not born-again righteous or perfect. Only the people who were raptured to heaven and returned with Jesus will be in their glorified state, plus those martyrs that are resurrected and glorified upon Christ's return (v.4). They counted in first resurrection (v.6).

The others, I would not classify as born-again righteous or perfect, but meet the qualification to be given rite of passage to enter the kingdom. So, a sizable percentage of millennials will already be in their glorified bodies. But those that survived the Great Tribulation without taking the mark of the beast will enter the millennium in their unglorified state. The group from the Judgment of Nations referred to as the sheep nations will not be in their glorified body yet (Matt. 25: 31-46).

So, Satan is absent, he is in prison. But what about the millions of falling angels that work for Satan? We have not read anywhere in Scripture that they were put in prison with Satan. So, we must conclude that they keep Satan's evil enterprise in business while Satan is in prison. If a person is not born-again from above, like a pig, nothing will prevent that person from heading to the mud, such behavior is programed in the soul.

Second, many new generations of humans will be born during the one-thousand millennium years. If a generation is 40 years, there will be 25 new generations. They are not born saved; they must accept Jesus as Savior and Lord just as we do today. Jesus ruling on earth from Jerusalem is their normal, it's no big thing to them. They were born into that way of life.

These generations will read about King Jesus arriving on earth with an army of saints and angels to topple the previous government, fight the war of Armageddon, and seize power to become the King. They will read how a bad angel named Satan was arrested and placed in prison and will be on parole shortly. All this will read like fiction, and they will watch movies on it as we watch old Western movies. Satan will seem attractive to some of them, and they will follow him instead of Jesus. Millions of these new millennials will follow Satan.

For this reason, Satan will be released from prison at the near end of the millennial age (Rev.20:3, 7). No sooner than Satan is out of prison he is back to his old tricks. He forms an army of rebels and sympathizers to attack the government.

This vast multitude of insurrectionists will converge on the Capital City, Jerusalem and try to storm the throne room of Jesus Christ. You could call this, Satan's last *hurrah*. Fire comes down out of heaven and consume his millions of human followers and Satan is thrown into hell, the burning lake of sulfur (Rev.20: 7-10). Satan has served his purpose and has met his final demise. The old fellow was faithful to his cause to the bitter end. The millions of angels and humans that serve his cause will share his eternal fate.

The final group of human followers that led the last uprising and are consumed with fire falling from heaven will be resurrected to face trial at the Final Judgment (see Volume 8).

CHAPTER 4

LIFESTYLE OF THE MILLENNIUM

The Millennium or Kingdom Age as it is at times called, is characterized by righteousness. To understand this coming age of righteousness from a distant, we must first understand the character and purpose of God in creation and redemption.

Frankly, the purpose of God in creation and redemption is the same; that is, to display His righteousness for His praise and glory. The heavenly bodies are signs, they convey God's message to us.[1] God's revelation of Himself is in two books: the book of nature and the book of holy Scriptures.

The Book of Nature

God displays His righteousness, objectively, in creation; it is the universal book that all created beings can see and understand, especially humans. As the architectural excellence of a building brings praise to the builder, the creation was designed to reflect God's glory, and bring praise and glory to Him.

The Psalmist looking at the planetary heavens made this declaration, "The heavens declare the glory of God; and the firmaments shows His handiwork" (Ps.19:1-2 NKJV). Because the message is universal, the Psalmist goes on to say, "Day by day utters speech, and night unto night reveals knowledge. There is no speech or language where their voice is not heard. Their line has gone out throughout all the earth, and their words to the end of the world"(vv.3-4 NKJV).

We earth dwellers are strategically located in the universe. We have front-row seats to observe the awe-inspiring wonder of the universe, and we have gotten good at it. We invented massive earth-based instruments, satellites, and other flying machines like Hubble and the James Webb Telescope that uncover for us the wonders of the heavens.

These smart machines have sent us jaw-dropping, eye-bulging, tongue stuttering images. These stunning images point us heavenward to the Creator, and move some of us to express our sentiments in words like, "How Great Thou Art." This song, made popular by George Beverly Shea and Cliff Barrows, expresses the author's devotion to the Creator for His creation. It is a tribute of praise and glory:

> O Lord my God, when I am in awesome wonder, consider all the worlds thy hands have made, I see the stars, I hear the rolling thunder, thy power throughout the universe display!
> Then sings my soul, my Savior God to thee; how great thou art, how great thou art....[2]

The author of "How Great Thou Art" was doing exactly what God intended creation to do—speak to humans of His righteous greatness and inspire them to praise and glory. It is for the same reason the book of Scripture was given.

The Book of Scripture

The Book of God's Word reveals His righteous character and redemption plan for us, humans; it teaches how we subjectively showcase God's redemptive works of righteousness to the whole universe to His praise and glory. The apostle Paul speaks of Christians showcasing God's graciousness, mercies, and righteousness to the world in the ages to come as follows:

> But because of his great love for us, God, who is rich in mercy, made us alive with Christ even when we were dead in transgression—it is by grace you have been saved. And God raised us up with Christ and seated us with him in the heavenly realms in Christ Jesus, in order that in the coming age he might show the incomparable riches of his grace, expressed in his kindness to us in Christ Jesus.... For we are God's handiwork, created in Christ Jesus to do good works, which God prepared in advance for us to do. (Eph.2:4-10).

The Millennium then is the absolute showcasing of God's righteousness through His Son and through those whom He has redeemed. His kingdom has literally come to earth in both the natural and spiritual sense. For the first time the God-Man is sitting as King on an earthly throne. He refused that position in His first advent. That is why Pilate, the Roman governor, did not find Him a threat and wanted to release Him. But Caiaphas and his cronies wanted Jesus dead, so they pushed Pilate to the decision they wanted (Matt.26:11-27; John 19:1-16).

Upon His *Second Advent*, Jesus returns to reign. After all opposing authorities have been put down, He will ascend the throne of David to reign as KING of Kings and LORD of Lords over the whole earth in righteousness and justice. But this includes a spiritual reign in the hearts of people as well.

As King, Jesus ends the rule of all gentile powers. This fulfills the prophecy that says, "the government shall be upon his shoulders…. And he will be called…Mighty God, Everlasting Father, Prince of Peace. Of the greatness of his government there will be no end…" (Isa.9:6-7).

The War of Armageddon not only ends the rule of gentile powers but also the end of all wars. The Prince of peace now reigns, and the earth is filled with the glory of God.

The millennium is fundamentally about the glory of God; it displays the righteous character of God to the children of men. God's throne is established in righteousness, truth, and justice (Psalm 97:2, 89:14). These attributes are foundational to His character and essential to His moral nature. God wants to display His essential character of righteousness to all creation through the human family, created in His image and likeness.

So, upon His return, Jesus will judge the world by His standard of truth, righteousness, and justice (Psalm 98:9).

These attributes are personified in Jesus Christ, the one who will sit as judge of all humans (John 5: 22-23; Rom.2:16).

Since the expulsion of humans from the paradise garden, there has not been a society or nation on earth that reflects righteousness to God's satisfaction. Humans are inherently depraved, and utterly incapable of rising to God's acceptable moral standard on their own (Rom.8:3-4). Humans need a Savior and the internal dwelling of the Holy Spirit to live up to God's standard. That is why the new law of God is written inwardly; it signals the reign of God in the inner sanctum (Jer.31:31-34; Heb.8:8-13; Rom.8:3-11).

Yet, humans want to do it their way, independent of God. That is the destructive pride that characterizes humanity from Eden to now. It is a pride that finds its root and origin in Satan himself. It has brought about his downfall, as well as the downfall of humans (Gen.3:1-6; Ezek.28:14-17; Isa.14:12-15). God wants to display His righteousness, not pride.

Within the display of divine righteousness are truth, justice, and mercy. Jesus is the very personification and standard of God's righteousness; He embodies these attributes of God. The very core of righteousness is justice, and justice cannot stand without truth. For that reason, humans raise their hands in a court of law and swear to *tell the truth and nothing but the truth, so help me God.* In essence, they call on God to help them speak the truth, and not be a false witness (Exod.20:16).

Despite the upheld hands before God and men and a sworn statement to tell the truth and nothing but the truth, people still give false testimony to abort justice.

But the One who sits on the throne in the millennial kingdom is the same One who sits on the bench of justice as the omniscient judge. He is truth personified. He said of Himself, "I am the way, the truth, and the life: no man comes to the Father, but by me" (John14: 6 KJV). You can only have perfect justice when a perfect judge sits on the bench.

The history of humans upon the earth has been one of war and discontent, because there can be no peace without justice. And there can be no justice without truth. Jesus is the personification of both. The prophet Micah echoes this core essential of divine righteousness when he said, He has shown you Oh man what doth the Lord requires of you, to do justly, to love mercy and to walk humbly before your God (Micah 6:8).

Because God wants human relationships to reflect justice, He has instituted human government to ensure justice in society (Gen.9:5-6; Exod.20:13; Rom.13:1-7). But justice must be administered not with cruelty but with mercy. Why?

Because mercy is another moral attribute of God; He uses mercy to restrain Himself dealing with us humans. Jesus said, "Blessed are the merciful: for they shall obtain mercy" (Matt.5: 9 KJV). Jesus rebuked the religious leaders of His day for their lack of mercy dealing with fellow humans (Luke 10:25-37).

One function of the Church in the world is to display the righteousness of God to the praise and glory of God. The apostle Paul expresses it this way, "And God raised us up with Christ and seated us with him in the heavenly realms in Christ Jesus, in order that in the coming ages he might show the incomparable riches of his grace, expressed in his kindness to us in Christ Jesus" (Eph.2:6-7).

Believers display the righteousness of God to the world as an alternate lifestyle to the glory of God. God intends the unregenerate world to look at the lifestyle of the people of God and say, *we want that*! That outcome has not been fully achieved, but the Church has not done badly. When Jesus left it was about 120 strong (Acts 1:15). Today, the number of Christians in the world has grown to over 3 billion.

The Millennium is a partial display of what the earth could have been if humans did not compromise with Satan in the paradise garden or at least if Israel did not reject Jesus. It is Israel's, second chance to accept the Messiah and for others to enjoy what our ancestral parents handed over to Satan.

It is worth emphasizing that the millennium is the ultimate display or showcasing of divine righteousness but with some old-world charms. In other words, this is not the new heaven and new earth promised, those will come later.

The millennium is one-step short of what earth would have been if humans did not partner with Satan, as stated earlier. If you have never sat on a throne before with a crown on your head, here is your chance. If you have toiled all your life to scratch out living to make too ends meet, that is over, the curse is lifted (Rom.8:18-15). Work remains but toiling for a living is no more.

The True Life of the Millennium

What truly characterizes life in the millennium? Other than God showcasing His righteousness on earth, what else there is? Oh, yes! Satan is in prison, the curse that was placed on creation at the Fall of man is lifted, and Jesus is at the head of government. These are major happenings that the earth has not seen since humans were expelled from Eden. What are some smaller things that make life truly grand during this kingdom age?

First, there will be true and equal justice under the law. We have already addressed this, so we need not say much more here. But know for sure that if you have never had or seen true justice all your life, now it is on full display. The earth is filled with the glory of God as the waters cover the seas.

Human history is characterized by slavery, holocaust, genocide, and war, among other atrocities. These things happen because the powerful dominate the weak and deprive them of their rights. These issues are covered under the six commandments that deal with human relationships. If there is no justice, there will be no peace! For this reason, among others, the millennium is marked by justice for all under the law. Justice is the essence of righteousness.

The Prophet Isaiah, speaking of the reign of the Christ during the His millennial kingdom said this, "Of the greatness of his government and peace there will be no end. He will reign upon the David's throne and over his kingdom, establishing and upholding it with justice and righteousness...forever" (Isa.9:7).

Second, there will be no lack but massive economic prosperity for all, globally. The United Nations has asserted that there is enough food for all upon earth, but greed causes some countries to be overfed, while others are starving. It will not be so in the millennium. There will be abundance for all. The desert places of the earth will come alive and productive. The fulness of life promised by our Lord will be fully realized (John 10:10). And the scourge that brings lack be forever gone.

So, if you never had anything, now you have everything; earth is back to its Edenic state. The earth and everything in it belong to God (Ps.24:1). He will distribute resources as sees fit. Of course, humans are free moral agents and still capable of sinning. And death, although conquered, will not be destroyed until after the millennium, at the final Judgment (Rev.20:11-15). But humans never had it better since Eden.

Third, the cessation or abolition of war will be permanent. Armageddon will be the final war fought before we enter the millennium. It will forever end Gentile rule on earth. Jesus will truly reign over the earth as the Prince or King of peace. "He will judge between the nations and will settle disputes for many peoples. They will beat swords into plowshares and their spares into pruning hooks. Nations will not take up sword against nations, nor will they train for war anymore" (Isa.2:4). Weapons of war will be transformed into agricultural equipment.

Nations today spend billions of dollars upon war machines and equipment, training for war, and fighting wars. And billions more upon security. And think of the millions of lives lost, property destroyed, and pain and suffering upon those that survive. Jesus tagged Satan as the one who comes to steal, kill, and destroy (John 10:10a). The Bible labels Satan as a murderer from the beginning; he was behind the first murder. It became evident from Cain killed his brother without penitence or remorse who inspired him (Gen.4:3-16). Cain was Satan's boy; like Judas, he was the son of perdition (John 17:12; 1 John 3:12). God Himself judged Cain and sentenced him for life.

Satan, the father of murder and the one who inspired Cain, will be confined to prison during the millennium. And what a difference it will make! No more war, just peace; prosperity is everywhere, and life flourishing as it was meant to be.

Fifth, even the animal kingdom will be at peace in the millennium. The Prophet Isaiah gives us this intelligence report on the animal kingdom, "The wolf will live with the lamb, the leopard will lie down with the goat, the calf and the lion and the yearling together; and a little child will lead them" (Isa.11:6).

The prophet goes on to say, "The cow will feed with the bear, their young will lie down together, and the lion will eat straw like the ox. The infant will play near the cobra's den, the young child will put its hand into the viper's nest" (vv7-8). "They will neither harm nor destroy on all my holy mountain, for the earth will be filled with the knowledge of the LORD as waters cover the sea" (v.9). All this is saying to us that nature will be kinder and gentler than it is now.

Sixth, the blessing of longevity of life will once again be realized. We often look at the life span of Old Testament people with skepticism because it is hard to accept that with the advance of science, especially medical technologies, the human life span though apparently longer, has gotten shorter from a biblical perspective. Without a doubt, there are contributing spiritual factors to the shorter life span, but that is not a domain of science so that explanation is dismissed by secular academia.

Once, theology was once called, the queen of the sciences, because it not only existed before them, it gave birth to them. Many of the institutions of higher learning were founded to train pastors and teachers (e.g., Harvard, Yale, Princeton). The Bible and theology teach that the Fall of man severely affected his original capabilities and curtail his longevity of life. But the Bible also teach that longevity of life will be regained.

The Prophet Isaiah addresses the longevity question of the millennial age: "Never again will there be in it an infant who live but a few days, or an old man who does not live out his years; the one who dies at a hundred will be thought a mere child; the one who fails to reach a hundred will be considered accursed" (Isa.65:20). This last clause suggest that death will be used as a punishment for sin in the sense that it is used in the fifth commandment for those who dishonor their parents, their longevity of life is shortened (Exod.20: 12).

Seven, sickness and disabilities will be no more. Sickness, disease, disabilities, and death are part of the curse. In as much as the curse will be lifted, death will stay around for a while until God has no more use for it. It is the last enemy to be destroyed (1Cor.15:24-25; Rev.20:11-15). The Word of God tells us, "For as in Adam all die, so in Christ all will be made alive" (v.22). Death will claim every child of Adam. But death does not have the last word. Jesus will raise everyone back to life, but they will not all go to the same destination (John 5:28).

But life will be flourishing and not plagued with sickness, disease, and disabilities in the millennium (Isa.33:24; Jer.30:17). The prophets speak to what we called disabilities: "In that day the deaf will hear the words of the scroll, and out of gloom and darkness the eyes of the blind will see" (Isa.29:18). The prophet goes on to say, "Then will the eyes of the blind be opened and the ears of the deaf unstopped. Then will the lame leap like deer, and the mute tongue shout for joy" (35:5-6).

Indeed the "Sun of Righteousness has risen with healing in His wings," as Malachi asserts (Mal.4:2). In righteousness, redemption brings wholeness and flourishing to the fallen creation. The millennium is the demonstration of that.

Eight, the millennium is characterized by overwhelming joyful living. Since the fall of man, life at its best is stressful. At its worst, it is hell. Even in wealthy, developed countries, the struggle of life for some is unbearable. But all that will be changed with the Son of God as the head of government.

With peace in people's hearts, peace with God, peace with neighbor, peace among nations and peace in the environment, Satan in prison, the wicked ceasing their troubling, goodwill and prosperity everywhere—the conditions are right for fulness of joy. God's will is being done on earth as in heaven.

Summary

The conditions of life during the millennium will be transformational, overwhelmingly joyful, and flourishing. It would take a very large volume to capture all blessings. This small volume can only give some significant highlights to give you a feel for what life will be like. Earth has never had it better since the Eden experience.

All who enter the millennium in their natural bodies will rare families and live their best lives. In fact, the population of the earth will grow exceeding because the conditions will be ideal for that (Jer.30;20, 31:29)

Those that enter the millennium in their resurrected or glorified bodies will not reproduce but they will be involved in just about everything else. Most glorified individuals will be in the administration and services of the government, such as kings, governors, mayors, Lords, justices, priests, and the like.

CHAPTER 5

THE GOVERNMENT OF THE MILLENNIUM

Overview

Like the human family, government is a divine institution, they both find their origin in God. The family is the first institution; it predates nation and government. Family turns into clan, clan into tribe, and tribe into nation. A nation is a big family with wider governance rules.

Government is the agreed mechanism to make the nation, the big family, work for the benefit of all or the common good. The divine mandate given to the first family in the *Paradise Garden* was, "Be fruitful and increase in number; fill the earth with your kind and subdue it. Rule over the fish in the sea, the birds in the sky and every living creature that moves on the ground" (Gen.1:27-28).

The authority given to the first couple was comprehensive; it includes the rule over marine life, the atmospheric heaven, and the birds that fly through it, the land and everything on it and moves upon it. They were given a kingdom to rule over, responsibility so grand, it later moved the Psalmist to rhetorical ask, what is mankind that God is so mindful of them, human beings that God cares about them? God crowned them with glory and honor and set them over His creation (Psalm 8:1-8).

The Creator gave them the intelligence to rule. They initially demonstrated their knowledge by naming things, classifying, and categorizing them (Gen.2:19-20). That is what science today refers to as taxonomy, naming and categorizing things.

One very important part of the mandate given to the man and the woman was to reproduce and fill the earth with their kind (Gen.1: 27-28). Every group is implied in the mandate: family, clan, tribe, nation, and government. As families increase, they take on new labels of identification. A nation is the largest group; it is all inclusive of families, clan, and tribes.

But another thing is implied in the mandate given to the man and the woman; they were given authority, and they were placed under authority. They were made accountable to the One who gave them their assignment. They were given the great privilege of leadership, but that awesome responsibility comes with accountability (Gen.2:8, 15-17).

The man and the woman violated divine law and were held to account. They proved irresponsible! Consequently, they were expelled from paradise as salves to the soil. They must now labor to live and raise a family until they die and return to the dust from which they were taken (Gen.3:1-19, 23-24).

But the story did not end there. God had a backup plan called, redemption (Gen.3:15). Most backup plans are not after-thoughts, they are put in place from the beginning, just in case something goes wrong. In God's plan, Jesus is the Lamb slain from the foundation of the world (John 1:29-31, 35-39; Rev.5:5-14, 13: 8). The plan was put in place from eternity, but its execution was done in time on Calvary (Gal.4: 4).

The Fall of a Race

The Fall of Man--from God's standard in paradise was not the fall of one person; it was the fall the whole human race. Adam, the father of the race, was a seed bag; the entire race was in him. The deficits he acquired in the debacle of the fall genetically affected all the seeds he carried. The apostle Paul reminds us that "sin entered the world through one man, and death through sin [and] in this way death came to all people, because all sinned" (Rom.5:12).

The sum of the matter is this—death and dying entered the human family through our ancestral parents, Adam and Eve; they contaminated the entire gene pool. The creation law is that everything produces after its kind (Gen.1:24-28).

Despite the deficit of being a carrier of death and dying, the creation mandate for the man and the woman is still: "Be fruitful and increase in number; fill the earth and subdue it" (Gen.1:28). The original intent of God is for humans to build families. Families become clans, tribes, and nations. But every person is a carrier of death and dying because we are all connected to the parents of the race. They ingested a deadly poison that altered their genetics and we are all affected.

Sin is a spiritual disease, but it produces the biological outcome of disease, dying, and death. This death and dying deficit manifested itself in Adam's first son, Cain. He murdered his brother without remorse. God tried him and gave him life sentence for his unrepentant brutality (Gen.4:1-16).

Cain's offspring tried to build a nation, but like their ancestral fathers, they refused to be accountable to God, and He destroyed them in the great flood of Noah's time (Gen.6-8).

God started over to build a righteous nation with the post-flood generation, but that ended with the Tower of Babel debacle (Gen.9-11). What was the problem? All these people were infected with the death and dying spiritual disease inherited from Adam and Eve. They were in a state of rebellion against God. Their sinful, deprave nature rendered them incapable of building a righteous society on their own. They needed divine help, but pride would not allow them to accept such help. They wanted to do it their own way, not God's way.

Going his own way independent of God, has been the history of humankind on the earth since his expulsion from the paradise garden. Despite the repeated failure of humankind, God has not given up on humans.

Yet again, God started to build a new nation with the man, Abraham. God's plan was to build a righteous nation with this one man, a nation that would be the head and not the tail, a model nation through whom He would bless all nations on earth. God made a covenant with Abraham (Gen.12:1-9).

The nation took the name of Abraham's grandson, Israel, a name given by God Himself. The rest of the Old Testament is about God dealing with this special people and what happened to them as they interacted with other nations.

Israel and the kingdom

Again, God intended Israel to be the model nation; He would be their God and King. They would be the conduit of His revelation and blessing to all nations. And through them the Messiah would come. But very early in Israel's history they objected to God being their King and opted for a king like the surrounding nations. They opted not for a theocracy but for a monarchy. Their first king, anointed by Samuel, was Saul. He was a disaster because he refused to be guided by God. God rejected him!

Israel's second king was David, a man after God's own heart. Under his leadership, the nation had its best days. But David was not a perfect man; he was greatly flawed.

His son Solomon began well as a wise king but ended poorly. His foreign wives turned his heart away from the Lord, and the nation went downhill soon after his death. It never regained its luster equal to the times of David and Solomon.

First, the nation split into two kingdoms: Northern with 10 tribes and Southern with two. Because of persistent idolatry, the Northern kingdom was taken captives to Assyria, and they never returned; these ten tribes are lost to history.

Second, the Southern Kingdom also became persistently idolatrous, and the best of their people were carried as exiles to Babylon by Nebuchadnezzar. The city was burnt, the walls knocked down, and the temple destroyed.

Third, after seventy years a remnant was allowed to return to rebuild the walls of Jerusalem and rebuild the temple (see Ezra and Nemiah). Despite the effort to rebuild, Israel never regained its former glory as in the days of David and Solomon.

Fourth, by the time Jesus was born, Israel was already an occupied nation again. This time the occupation was by the

Romans. The Messiah was their last hope to fulfill the covenant promises and restore them to the number one nation God wanted them to be. But it had to be done God's way! To add insult to injury, they rejected the Messiah and had the Romans crucified Him. The Messiah predicted that would result in the destruction of their cities and temple and their dispersion.

Fifth, that destruction and dispersion took place in AD 70 when the Roman army destroyed Jerusalem, burnt the temple, killed thousands of Jews, and carried thousand more off as prisons of war. Judaism as it existed during the time of Jesus, permanently ended. Modern day Judaism is a reinvention without the City of David (Jerusalem), without the temple, without the Ark of the Covenant, without sacrifice, without the priesthood, and without the Shekinah light of glory.

The Important Question

Has God cast away His covenant people, Israel? The answer is, no! Israel continues to play a pivotal role in God's end-time program, as the apostle Paul clearly asserts in Romans 9-11. The promises God made under the Abrahamic, Mosaic, Davidic, and the New Covenant will be fulfilled largely through the nation of Israel and the Messiah, Jesus Christ.

First, God promised to regather Israel from among the nations He scattered them and bring them back to their covenant land (Ezek.37:13-15). We have witnessed this regathering most vividly since the turn of the 20th Century under the handwork of Zionism. This mushroomed with the miraculous rebirth of the modern State of Israel.

The regathering will be brought to its completion with the Second Advent of the Christ as discussed in Volume 6 of this series. That is necessary for two main reasons. (1) There are still strong forces at work in the world bent on getting rid of God's first covenant people. And (2) there are *the ten lost tribes of Israel* that must be sought out. They are not lost to God. But not all Israelites are of the covenant, and there are Jews who are unaware of their identity. And there are those who mistakenly think they are Jews and are not. The Messiah is omniscient in knowledge and will determine who are the covenant people.

Second, Jesus will return in time to rescue Israel from annihilation by Gentiles powers; He will put down all opposition to His authority (Rev.19:11-21,20:1-6) (See Vol.6).

Third, Jesus will judge the nations and establish His rule or government on earth from Israel's capital city, Jerusalem (Isa.9:6-7; Matt.25:31-46). The fulfillment of these promises answers the question of the disciples to Jesus hour before His ascension, "Lord, are you at this time going to restore the Kingdom to Israel?" Jesus answered, "It is not for you to know the times or dates the Father has set by his own authority..." (Acts 1:6-7). The strong implication here is that the restoration of the kingdom to Israel was yet future, in God's own time. This conclusion is supported by many OT and NT scripture passages (e.g., Isa.9:6-7).

The Restored Kingdom

First, the restored kingdom will be a monarchial-theocracy. On the one hand, Jesus Christ is a member of the Godhead, so He is God; that makes His government a theocracy. On the other hand, Jesus Christ returns to earth to rule as KING of Kings and LORD of Lords (Rev.19:16). That makes Him the Monarch to whom all regent kings, lords, and governors are responsible.

Israel was a theocracy before it became a monarchy under their first king, Saul. Theocracy was God's preferred model of government for them. But the nation wanted a king and God sanctioned it. Israel's best years as a monarchy were under King David and his son King Solomon, David's successor. After Solomon, the nation declined to gradual extinction.

Second, God promised that one of David's sons would sit on his throne, and rule over his kingdom perpetually (2 Sam.7:14; 1Chron.17:7-14 NKJV). Note verse 14, "And I will establish him in My house and in My kingdom forever; and his throne shall be established forever." We know this promise has not yet come to pass, nor is it a reference to king Solomon. We know from Scripture that this promise will ultimately is fulfilled in Jesus Christ, the Messiah. He is from the linage of David and is often referred to as the Son of David (Matt.21:1-16; Luke 2:4-7).

Third, other prophecies speak of Jesus Christ, the Messiah, as a human and divine person, not only as Son of God and Son of Man, but as the Son of David that will sit on His throne and rule forever (Isa.7:13-17, 9:6-7). The first passage is addressed to the "house of David" (7:13) and identifies the Messiah as a male child born of a Virgin and is named, "Immanuel" (7:4) which means, "God with us" and directly points to the Messiah who is Jesus of Nazareth, the Son of the blessed Virgin Mary (Matt.1: 21-25). Now, look at the second passage (Isa.9: 6-7).

It also speaks of the Messiah in both human and divine terms: "Mighty God, Everlasting Father, Prince of Peace." The Messiah is the One who will have this responsibility of government; He will sit on the throne of David, and rule over his kingdom forever. All this will be the doings of the LORD of Hosts (v.7).

Fourth, the New Testament (NT) also speaks of the Messiah as the Son of David, as one that would sit on David's throne and rule over David's kingdom forever. Note well that it speaks of Him as David's Son before His birth, during His birth, and after:

- Before Jesus was conceived in the womb of the blessed Virgin Mary, the angel Gabriel said to her, "And behold, you will conceive...and bring forth a Son, and shall call His name Jesus. He will be great, and will be called the Son of the Highest; and the Lord God will give Him the throne of His father David. And He will reign over the house of Jacob forever, and of His kingdom there will be no end" (Luke 1:31-33 NKJV).

- Joseph and Mary went to Bethlehem, the city of David to be registered in a census because he was of the house and lineage of David. While they were there, Mary gave birth to baby Jesus (Luke 2:1-7 NKJV).

- The angel's announcement to the shepherds in the field said, "Do not be afraid, for behold, I bring you good tidings of great joy which will be to all people. For there is born to you this day in the city of David a Savior, who is Christ the Lord..." (Luke 2:8-18 NKJV).

- At the dedication of Jesus in the temple, the blessed Holy Spirit revealed to Simeon that this child is the Messiah (Luke 2:22-35 NKJV).

- The Prophetess Anna confirmed that Jesus is the Messiah, the Redeemer of Israel (vv.36-38).

Did Jesus of Nazareth sit on any earthly throne and rule over Israel or any nation during His first advent? The answer is, no! Did He have the responsibility of government upon His shoulders? No! Did He rule over David's kingdom? No! Instead, He died on a cross as the Savior of the world (John 3:16).

Therefore, these prophecies about Him sitting on David's throne and ruling over Israel and the world are yet future. They will happen upon His second advent, when He comes to reign in what is referred to as the "millennium" (Rev.19:11-16, 20:1-6). This is the clear teaching of the Scripture. What will be the nature of His government?

The Nature of Christ's Government

First, we have already established that the government of the Christ will be a monarchial-theocracy. But some people would see that as almost contradictory. Why? Throughout history governments were normally one or the other, not both. That is true, when speaking on a purely human level, not divine. The divine is always naturally and supernaturally skewed.

We cannot fit the operations of God into a framework that is purely human. God cannot be categorized and restricted by human boundaries. His government is a theocracy because it is under the rubric of the blessed Holy Trinity. But of course, the visible face of operation is Jesus Christ, the KING of Kings.

It bears the visible elements of a monarchy, but it is fundamentally a theocracy (Isa.9:6-7). From the time of Samuel, that's what God wanted for Israel and the whole earth, a theocracy. And when we pray, "thy kingdom come, thy will be done on earth as it is in heaven," that's what we are praying for—a theocracy, whether we are conscious of it or not.

Second, KING Jesus will not be ruling alone upon His return. There will be many regent kings, Lords, and officials in His administration all over the world. For that reason, He returns to earth as KING of Kings and LORD of Lords and with many crowns on His head. He returns in the company of a massive army of saints and angels (Rev.19:11-16). They are all regent leaders and will be answerable the KING of Kings.

Third, the seat of the millennial kingdom will be Jerusalem, the City of David, the place of Christ's throne, referred to as the throne of David (Isa.9:7). Christ ascended to heaven from the Mount of Olives overlooking the City of Jerusalem, and He will return to that very location (Acts 1: 9-12; Zech.14: 1-9).

Upon His return, Israel will fully embrace Yeshua as their Messiah which will instantly give Israel most favored nation status. This is the nation that God said would be the head and not the tail. But their disobedience caused them to be deposed and maltreated by gentile powers throughout the centuries, to the brink of annihilation. But God's covenant promises to them must be fulfilled, and that is why they are regathered from among the nations back to Israel, their covenant land. Gentile rule ends with the return or second advent of the Christ.

So, the seats of government will not be New York, Washington, DC, London, Paris, Rome, or any city other than Jerusalem. Not all nations and cities will be given the rite of passage to enter the millennial kingdom of the Christ. The judgment of nations will determine which nations enter the millennial kingdom (Matt.25:31-46). The whole world will look to Jerusalem, the capital city of the earth.

If Satan could, he would prevent Jesus from coming here to reign. Satan knows Jerusalem will be the seat of government for Messiah's worldwide rule, and that is why he fights so hard over the centuries to make Jerusalem his city. The Antichrist will be defeated in Jerusalem as Jesus descends from heaven to liberate Israel from annihilation. It is Satan's preemptive strike to occupy Jerusalem before the Messiah comes to claim it and to reign.

Fourth, the millennial kingdom of the Christ is one of righteousness and justice. "Of the greatness of his government and peace there will be no end. He will reign on David's throne and over his kingdom, establishing and upholding it with justice and righteousness forever" (Isa.9:7). One Scripture says, He will rule with a rod of iron which means the rule of law will be strictly enforced (Isa.11:3-5).

Yet, mercy and compassion constitute the very nature of Christ. But not one will be able to manipulate the law or take advantage of the weak as it was during the times of the gentiles. Satan will not be around for people to blame their behavior on him. No one will be able to say, the devil made me do it.

Fifth, the millennial kingdom will be most glorious. In His high priestly prayer, Jesus asked the Father to restore the glory he divested Himself of to become incarnate. He also prayed for His followers to be where He is to behold His glory (John 17: 1-5, 22-24). What is "the glory" spoken of here?

On one hand, it is brightness. The sun, moon, and stars differ in glory (brightness). On the other hand, it is all that a king has that makes him great: the size of his kingdom, the power of his army, his personal wealth, the wealth of his kingdom, and how well his people live. When the Queen of Sheba beheld the glory of Solomon's kingdom, she fainted. She exclaimed that the half was never told to her (1Kings10:1-7). But Jesus is greater than Solomon in every sense. Solomon ruled over one little nation, Jesus will rule over the whole earth. His kingdom is universal; it will eclipse Solomon's kingdom in glory.

In Psalm 24: 8-10 the Lord is referred to as the King of glory, a mighty warrior, several times. Christ is depicted as a mighty warrior returning to earth on a milk white stallion with the armies of heaven following (Rev.19:11-21). His victory over the Antichrist's armies in the Armageddon War depicts Him as a mighty warrior also (Isa.63:1-6). His glory in terms of brightness will eclipse the heaven lights (Isa.24:23).

Sixth, the millennial reign of the Christ will be the most joyous time earth has seen since humans were expelled from the *Paradise Garden* (Gen.3:22-24). The curse is lifted off creation, there is global cessation from wars, the economy has flourished, everybody is prospering, the devil is in prison, and even the animals are at peace with each other. They are not vicious toward each other anymore. People are now able to live out the fulness of their days. *Happy days are here again,* and this is just the beginning, because better is still yet to come.

Seventh, sickness and disease are permanently removed. With the removal of the curse from creation, sickness and disease are no longer part of human experience (Isa.33:24).

Since the fall of man, the greater share of life's unhappiness come from suffering resulting from sickness and disease. Sickness and disease are related to the consequential outcome of the fall of humans in the paradise garden, including the resulting curse placed upon creation. With the glorification of the people of God, the lifting of the curse, and the King of the kingdom is on earth to reign, sickness and disease are no more.

Suffering used to be referred to as the Christian's Achilles heel, because its presence was most baffling to explain to the critics of the faith. The average Christian could not explain how a good, loving, benevolent, and all-powerful God could allow His creation to be marred with suffering, and He appears helpless to do anything about it. The Christian God must be either not loving, or not omnipotent, the critics argued.

Without a plausible explanation to suffering, Christians take comfort in the cross of Christ. For if that is God dying in the person of Jesus Christ in our place on that cross, then we are not alone in our sufferings. He shares our human plight and is indeed touched with our infirmities (Isa.53; Heb.4:15-16). But with the millennium, Christ has come to dwell with us and suffering and disease are permanently removed (Rom.8:22-30).

Summary

The millennial reign of the Christ is the literal kingdom of God of earth. It is the kingdom Christians have been praying in the Lord's Prayer to come. It is what Jews have been praying and looking for, the restoration of the Davidic kingdom (Acts 1:6-8). Both Jews and Christians have much vested in the coming of the kingdom with the Messiah, who is Jesus of Nazareth.

With the millennium, both Jews and Gentiles get much more than they have been praying for. We receive the perfect the world we could not bring about with our human genius minus God. With the kingdom God here in all its glory, we the people of God can live out our God given potentials.

The millennium reflects the ideal world both Jews and Gentiles want but without Jesus; they cannot have one without the other. As good as the millennial kingdom is, it is not the new heaven and the new earth God promised, that will come later.

CHAPTER 6
WORSHIP DURING THE MILLENNIUM

The Centrality of Worship

Worship is central to the Kingdom of God and will always be; the millennial kingdom, therefore, will retain that centrality of worship. Anywhere Jehovah God and created beings meet, worship is a paramount and a necessary protocol. This was true in the *Paradise Garden* and remained true after humans were expelled from *Paradise* (Gen.3:7-10, 4:1-12).

Noah was a worshipping man with his family before and after the great flood. For that reason, Noah found grace in the sight of God and offered sacrifice to God (Gen.6:17-8, 7:1-5, 8: 20-22). The worship of God set Noah apart from everyone else of his generation. His life of righteousness bore witness that his generation deliberately chose to defy and dishonor God, and the flood was the judgment of God upon them. Wicked people do worship, but they often worship the creature and not the Creator (Rom.1:1-32).

Abraham was also a worshipping man with his clan; he frequently built altars and sacrificed just about everywhere he went (Gen.12:1-3,8,13:1-4,18, 14:17-20). He must have learned this habit of worshipping God before he was called to leave his idolatrous surrounding to a new environment. There must have been something about him that drew him to God and God to him. His love of worship distinguished him from others.

There is no greater activity created beings can be engaged in than the worship of God. Worship is what God expects from humans and angels, and perhaps all others in their own way (Ecc.12:13-14; Rom.12:1-2; Rev.5:6-14, 15:1-8,19:1-10).

Worship appears to be the food of God, and all beings were created for worship. Loving worship fulfills the true purpose of human beings (Ecc.12:13-14; John 4:21-24). The apostle Paul indicates that the giving of ourselves to God in worship is our reasonable service, by it we come to know the true and perfect will of God (Rom.12:1-2). Worship satisfies the longing of the human heart and fills the aching void of the inner sanctum.

Scripture presents humans and angels as worshipping creatures of God in heaven and earth (Isa.6:1-7; Rev.4:1-11,5: 8-14). God never objects to receiving sincere creaturely worship, but strongly forbids creature worshipping creature or any created objects (Exod.20:1-7; Deu.6:4-19).

Noah, Abraham, Isaac, and Jacob were worshippers of God. God brought Israel to Sinai to teach them how to be a true worshipping community all the days of their lives. The Law given by God includes a worship system reflecting God's standard of worship. God does not accept worship that deviates from the standard He established. Two of Aaron's sons were sternly rebuked to death for their deviation from God's standard of worship (Lev.10:1-20).

Later in Israel's history, the High Priest Eli and his two sons, Hophni and Phineas who were priests under Eli, were all severely disciplined by God. They compromised God's standard of worship and dishonored God. These boys profaned God's sanctuary and disgraced His holy name. Eli proved to be a permissive father; he failed to correct his sons appropriately. For that reason, they all died the same day, most tragically (1 Sam.3:11-14, 4:1-22). The discipline of God is not joyous.

The New Testament (NT) also shows several examples of worship abuse, where God steps in to exercise discipline. There is the case of Ananias and his wife Sapphira who were disciplined to death in the public worship (Acts 5: 1-11). The church at Corinth was disciplined for many abuses including that of the Lord's Supper (1Cor.11:27-34). When we fail to discipline ourselves and church leaders fail to discipline, God steps in to exercise discipline and that could be as severe as physical death, as the preceding passage reveals.

God made it clear that He is a jealous God and does not give or share His glory with any other. The first four commandments safeguard God's honor and glory from idolatry (Exod.20:1-8). What is idolatry? It is embracing false gods and false worship.

The other six of the Ten Commandments are to protect God's honor in human relationships (vv.12-17). The dispersion of Israel among the nations from off their covenant land had to do with idolatry (Deut.28:1-68). Idolatry is about worship: the who, the what, the how, and the time of worship.

Worship, Judaism and Jesus

By the time of Jesus' ministry, Judaism had developed into a false worship system. Jesus confronted its leaders, but they resisted Him strongly. He tried very hard to correct and clean up the system, as symbolized by His cleansing of the temple. But His efforts produced no positive outcome of change. Instead, they hated Him the more and sought to kill Him.

The religious leaders rejected Him strongly. Eventually, they had Him arrested on false charges and convinced the Roman governor to crucify Him for sedition against the state. But before His death, Jesus scathingly denounced the corrupted religious system, and prophesied its destruction (Matt.24: 1-2).

The Roman Legion finally drove the last nail into the coffin of that false religious system in AD 70 when Jerusalem and the temple were destroyed. Israel fought back valiantly but they lost the war. Thousands of Jews were killed and thousands more carried off as prisoner of war. That permanently ended traditional Judaism, as it was known and practiced back then.

Judaism reinvented itself, but it remains a false worship system to the 21st Century. Why? The worship standard was hand down to Israel from God to Moses at Mount Sinai; Israel believed that worship could not be authentically practiced without the Tabernacle or the Temple, sacrifice, priesthood, the Ark of the Covenant, and the Shekinah glory of God. With the destruction of the Temple in AD 70, Israel loss these six things. That means the divine model and standard of worship was lost. Modern day Judaism is man's reinvention.

But even if Judaism had retained these six things, because of Israel's rejection of Yeshua (Jesus) as the Christ (Messiah), their worship would still be false. The entire worship system given by God through Moses pointed to Jesus Christ and is useless if He is out of the picture. The book of Hebrews is a commentary on the significance of Judaism worship system.

By virtue of the death and resurrection of Jesus Christ, the entire Levitical system comes to an end: the old ceremonial laws, priesthood, sacrifice, temple, and so on. A New Covenant is in effect with the Lamb of God as the sacrifice, a new priestly order with Jesus as high priest, and a new sanctuary. God is not going back to this old system, not now, not ever. That is why it is misleading to think the sacrificial system will be reinstated in the millennium (more on this later).

If you point out the falsehood of this reinvented religious worship system today, especially to orthodox Jews, you will be denounced as antisemitic, and you too will face crucifixion. It is an uncomfortable truth. But don't get me wrong, Judaism is culturally rich, sophisticated, and colorful with great benefits. But without Yeshua, the Messiah, it does not measure up to God's acceptable standard of worship. It has no sacrifice for sin. Messianic Judaism is acceptable to God; it embraces Yeshua.

The way to God is through Christ alone (John 14:4-14). This is a biblical truth, but not a politically correct statement. And because it is the truth, it is worth repeating for emphasis. Any worship system that rejects Jesus Christ will not lead you to eternal life; it will lead to destruction (Matt.7:13-14; John 3:14-21). If Christ is not Savior and Lord in that worship system, I strongly warn you, get out of it now!

During the *Second Advent* of the Christ, all that Israel lost and more, will be restored in the millennium (not the return of the old system). At that time, the spiritual blindness that Israel suffers during the Church Age will be lifted (Rom.10:1-22). They will see clearly that Yeshua whom their ancestors rejected, and crucified is indeed the true Messiah of Israel. Zechariah writes, "They will look on me, the one they have pierced, and they will mourn for him as one mourns for an only child and grieve bitterly as one for a firstborn son" (Zech.12:10).

On that day, Israel will embrace Jesus Christ as their Messiah, Savior, Lord, and King. Then all the covenant related promises will be fulfilled for God is faithful and keeps His word. In other word, Israel will embrace the New Covenant with Messiah; Messiah is not going back to the old system. With these truths in mind, we now turn to discuss the Third Temple.

Building the Third Temple

There is much debate today among Christian and Jewish Bible scholars concerning the rebuilding of the Third Temple in Jerusalem on the Temple Mount. But there is no conscientious among Christians or Jews on the matter. But there are movements and organizations dedicated to the rebuilding of the Third Temple. Religious Jew believe the Temple must be in place before the Messiah comes. In an article in Jewish Voice, October 07, 2022, Dr. Randall Price asserts:

> Since 1987, when the Temple Movement began preparations for the rebuilding of the Third Temple, efforts to see this become a reality in the 21st century have been slowly progressing. While modern Israel and a large percentage of the Jewish people throughout the Diaspora are secular, Orthodox Jews do not believe these people will play a role in the rebuilding of the Temple since it is a spiritual work. It

is Orthodox Jews who revived the Sanhedrin, the religious body that supervised the halachic (legal) issues related to the Temple and who intend to see it rebuilt in a proper way.[1]

Dr. Price goes on to say, "The importance to Orthodox Jews of rebuilding the Temple lies in its role in the redemption of the world, which they believe can only take place once the Temple is rebuilt."[2]

The problem here is that Orthodox Jews will not have the time to evangelize the world when Messiah returns, it will be too late then. Because of their ancestors' rejection of Jesus, the Messiah, the Church was raised up by Jesus Christ Himself and assigned the task of evangelizing the world with the gospel (Matt.16:13-20, 28:18-20).

So, the Orthodox belief that they will be evangelizing the world for the Messiah when He comes is a false notion. This false notion is rest upon the false antecedent notion that Yeshua (Jesus) is not the Messiah in keeping with their first century ancestors who rejected and crucified Jesus. Frankly, when Messiah returns, Jews will be the primary group that needs to be evangelized.

God Himself has made preparation for the evangelization of Israel. He will appoint 144,000 Messianic Jews to preach to Israel and Jews globally during the Great Tribulation period. That is after the Church is raptured from earth to heaven (Rev.7:1-17, 14:1-5). The grim truth is that Jews who reject Jesus as Messiah, cannot do the work of evangelizing fellow Jews. The evangelist must first come to faith in Jesus before he is qualified to witness (John 3:1-7, 14-16). And salvation from sin is only available through Jesus alone (Acts 4:12).

So, the rebuilding of the Third Temple is taken seriously by Orthodox Jews and some evangelical Christians. There is even an organization dedicated to that purpose. It is called "Temple Mount Faithful," directed by Gershon Salomon.[3] *Why is the rebuilding of the Third Temple so important?*

First, to Orthodox Jews, it is necessary for the redemption of the world. But that is a mistaken premise, as already stated.

Second, it is important to some evangelical Christians for two different reasons: 1) it is the fulfillment of certain biblical prophecies, and 2) it is central to worship in the millennial kingdom of the Christ. But the evangelical premise could also be false. As stated earlier, temple structure for the worship of God is an Old Covenant concept. It is one of the reasons Jesus prophesied its destruction.

While a building is convenient for worship, it does not hold the place of centrality under the New Covenant (John 4:21-24). It is where two or three people come together in the name of Jesus that holds centrality under the New Covenant.

In as much as this writer believes there will be a Third Temple—it won't be for the centrality of worship reason. No building: stone, brick, steel, wood or of other material will hold the place of centrality in worship under the New Covenant. In the religious psyche of Orthodox Jews, it might be central because that is all they know, but for Christians and Messianic Jews that is not so. The true temple is the spiritual one (Eph.2:19-22; 1Peter 2: 4-10).

For Christians a building is convenient but not necessary for the worship God; the human body is God's temple (Rom.12:1-2; 1Cor.6:19-20; 2Cor.6:14-18). Jesus asserts that where two or three people come together in His name, He is present among them (Matt.18:20). He also said that God is spirit and they that worship Him must do so in Spirit and in truth (John 4:19-24).

There are several perspectives for the rebuilding of the Third Temple. One is the fulfillment of prophecy argument. For example, Ezekiel speaks extensively about a temple which some scholars see as the future millennial temple, while others do not see it as the eschatological Third Temple at all.

Ezekiel prophesied to Israel during the Babylonian captivity. What would Jews in captivity miss the most? Answer, the temple! The temple was the center of Jewish life back in Israel. So, it is natural to have memories and visions of it, or to look forward to the day when the exile is over, and the temple is rebuilt. And that did happen; the Second Temple was rebuilt under Zerubbabel and the wall was rebuilt under Nemiah.

The question is whether Ezekiel's vision and prophecies about a temple are applicable to the Second Temple (now past) or the Third Temple which is yet future. It is hard to be dogmatic on which is the right answer. But this much we know, there will be a Third Temple in the millennial kingdom, but it will not be as significant as Jews and some Christians make of it. Yet, worship is central to the millennial kingdom. Let's unpack this.

Worship in the Theocratic Kingdom

The millennial kingdom of the Christ is a theocratic government which means worship is central to its operation. The driving force at the heart of secular nation States today is economics or money. The Bible calls it, the unrighteous mammon. The devotion given to money is akin to the worship once given to God in houses of worship. The love of money is the new national god and the new idolatry. Everybody worships but bows down at different altars. Like the kingdom of God, Satan's kingdom is about worship (Matt.4:8-10; Rev.13:4-8,15-17).

For that reason, apostate religion (Religious Babylon(RB) and the monetary systems of this world (Economic Babylon(EB) are almost identical. Compare Revelation 17 (RB) and 18 (EB).

It is not coincidental that the American dollar has written on it, "In God We Trust." When that was first written, the nation wanted to assert its Jewish-Christian values. But now the nation has long departed from those biblical values into nothing short of a pagan culture, so the object of the nation's worship is no longer the God of the Bible but the money itself.

That is where the once powerful Christian West now finds itself in this postmodern, post-Christian era. The grounding biblical, moral values that once served as cultural guardrails and landmarks are uprooted and replaced. Depravity, debauchery, and unbridled moral decadence eat away at the nation's soul.

The millennial kingdom will not be driven by economics, but the nations of the world will experience prosperity as never before, no more crime in the streets, no more wars between nations, no exorbitant healthcare budget because sickness and disease will be no more. Worship will be central to all nations, cities, and Jerusalem earth's capital. Pilgrimages will be made year after year to Jerusalem (Isa.66:20-23; Zech.14:16-21).

Congregate Worship

Congregate worship is the preferred way of God; this is evident from the *Paradise Garden* narrative. God would come down at a certain time to meet with His family in their garden home. But one day they did not show up for meeting and God went looking for them (Gen.3:7-13).

It is also evident that some form of congregate worship continued with the generation of Cain and Able after the expulsion of their parents from the *Paradise Garden* (Gen.4:4-5). Congregate worship appears to continue for Noah and his family, and from Abraham onward. God looked to the man as the priest of the family (Gen.18:17-19).

Under Moses' leadership, congregate worship became the established worship standard. God wanted to dwell among His people. For these reasons, God gave Moses the architectural plans for the Tabernacle and commanded him to build a sanctuary that He may dwell among His people. God also gave Moses the plans for the furnishings, the priesthood, the regulations for sacrifices, and the complete Israelite's worship system (Exod.25:1-8)). God sets the standard of worship.

When the Tabernacle was finished and dedicated, God came down to dwell with His people (Exod.40:34-38). The same is true of Solomon's Temple, when it was dedicated, the glory of God came down and fill the house of God (2Chron.7:1-4). There was never a happier time in Israel's history.

The congregational worship system continued until it was interrupted with the Babylonian captivity. This happened because the nation backslid, and the glory of God departed.

After decades of servitude in Babylon, a remnant returned, and the *Second Temple* was built under Zerubbabel, according to the book of Ezra. It was nothing in glory compared to Solomon's Temple. But at least, corporate worship resumed in Israel. By the time of Jesus, Israel was worshipping in the magnificent *Herodian Temple*. The external rituals of worship had improved but the system had become corrupt and ungodly. Jesus tried to fix it, but the religious leaders strongly resisted Him, rejected Him, and finally had Him killed.

But before His death, Jesus sat on the Mount of Olives, overlooking Jerusalem and predicted the utter destruction of the Jewish Temple and the entire corrupted worship system. It continued in its corrupted form until A.D.70 when the Romans destroyed Jerusalem and the Temple, as predicted by Jesus in His Olivet discourse (Matt.24:1-2). That ended the corrupted worship system denounced by Jesus. Until the writing of this book, no temple has been built in Israel to replace the Herodian Temple. But there will be a *Third Temple,* perhaps, by the Second Advent of the Christ. Others believe the Church is it.

The Church as the New Temple

When a worship system becomes corrupted, it ceases to represent the God of the Bible for He is Holy. When worship became persistently corrupted under Eli, the glory of God departed from Israel. But God did not leave Himself without a witness or worship system that meets His standard. Eli and his sons died, and the Ark taken, but God raised up Samuel.

In Jeremiah's time, God sent foreign armies to destroy Jerusalem and the temple. When Israel rejected Jesus their Messiah, Jesus established the Church as the new worship system to take over the assignment of world evangelization that was intended for Israel (Matt.16:13-20; 28:18-20).

Jesus established a new worship system unlike the one headed by Scribes and Pharisees. He denounced that system and prophesied its destruction (Matt.24:1-2). The old worship system depended on the elaborate, stationary structure of temple, priesthood, and animal sacrifices. It was ritualistically burdensome, corrupt, and void of spiritual life.

The leaders of Judaism resisted change. They vehemently rejected Jesus and had Him put to death. But before His death Jesus had no choice but to replace the old with a new worship system, the Church. We have a preview insight of the new form of worship from Jesus' conversation with the Samaritan woman (John 4:19-26).

The woman said to Jesus, "Sir, I perceive that you are a prophet. Our ancestors worshiped on this mountain [Mt. Gerizim], but you Jews claim that the place where we must worship is in Jerusalem" (vv.19-20). Remember, Samaritans and Jews were not in good relationship. Samaritans were not welcome to worship at the Temple in Jerusalem. Jesus replied:

> Woman, believe me, a time is coming when you will worship the Father neither on this mountain nor in Jerusalem. You Samaritans worship what you do not know; we worship what we know, for salvation is from the Jews. Yet a time is coming and has now come when the true worshippers will worship the Father in the Spirit and in truth, for they are the worshippers the Father seeks. God is spirit, and his worshippers must worship in Spirit and in truth (vv.21-24).

Jesus was pointing the woman to a new worship system, one without walls, one not limited to time and choice location, one welcoming of all nationalities, races, and cultures, one not driven by dead rituals but by vibrant, dynamic worship in the Holy Spirit. Jesus was pointing to the Church He would build, and the gates of hell would not prevail against it (Matt.16:18).

The NT Church was born on the Day of Pentecost as the new people of God, the new worship community, empowered by the blessed Holy Spirit (Acts 2:1-47; 1Peter 2: 9-10).

In addition to being a worship community, the Church has an assignment to evangelize the world (Matt.28:19-20; Acts 1:8). She has been running with the good news of salvation since Pentecost to the far-flung regions of the earth.

The Church is God's new worship center made up of people, a community, a fellowship where the blessed Holy Spirit dwells (Eph.2:19-22). Yes, this community of people use the shiny building on the corner as an instrument of ministry, but it is not the Church that Christ said He would build, and the gates of hell will never prevail against it. The people are that community.

Millennial worship will permeate every region of the earth. The earth will be fill with the glory of God as the water covers the sea. The whole world will be God's sanctuary. Will there be material structures such as we now worship out of? Of course, they will be in every village, every hamlet, town, city, metropolis, and especially in Jerusalem where the seat of government will be located. There the KING of Kings will sit on *the Throne of David*. Zion will always be the chief worship center. In the Hebrew mindset that must include the Temple.

It is doubtful the Third Temple will be the one Ezekiel extensively describes. Jerusalem with be the Capital of the theocratic government and it will revolve around worship not economics like Washington D.D., New York, London, or Paris. The only city on earth that was designed for worship is Vatican City, but it is likely to become the headquarters of the apostate church. Like Jesus, Satan has a global plan; he wants to rule the world and be worshiped (Matt.4:8-11; Rev.13::1-18, 17:1-17).

Satan is jealous of Jesus, he imitates Jesus, and tries to preemptively setup his worship system before Jesus arrives, so he surrounds Jerusalem with armies to fight Jesus. God will destroy the apostate church and Jesus will deal with Satan's army in Jerusalem upon His arrival (Rev.19:11-21; Isa.63:1-6).

The Vatican City is a faint idea of what the seat of Jesus' government will physically looks like (Isa.9:7). But it will be designed for massive worship. It will constantly accommodate worshippers on pilgrimage from all over the world paying homage to the KING of Kings and LORD of Lords. It is the place where Jesus receives all the Kings under His rule all over the world. They must come to Jerusalem at least once each year.

Animal Sacrifice Reinstated?

With the building of the Third Temple, will animal sacrifice be reinstated? To answer this question, we must look at two issues: 1) the necessity for a Third Temple and animal sacrifice, and 2) what the totality of Scriptures teaches.

First, the Temple issue. Is a Third Temple necessary, and for whom, and for what? Does God really need a brick-and-mortar building? When we consider the sum of scripture passages correctly, the short answer is no! that is clear from the previous section that NT worship is not tied to a building.

For what group of people does this Third Temple have primary significance? The answer is, for backslidden Israel who refused to change when Jesus corrected their corrupted worship system. Instead, they rejected their Messiah and had the Roman executed Him. The infant church gave them an opportunity to correct this horrible mistake (Acts 2:14-41, 3:11-26, 4:1-21, 7:1-60, 9:1-21)

But rather than admit to their mistake and repent, they covered up the resurrection of the Christ and perpetuated a lie to the world (Matt.28:1-15). Their children and the generations following did the same, covered up the resurrection of the Christ. The lie continues to this day (21st century). The facts of history are available to everyone, but Jews chose to continue the rejection of the Messiah, believe, and practice a lie.

The dominos began to fall with Israel's persistent rejection and elimination of Jesus. Then comes the prophecy against the Temple and its destruction by the Romans in AD 70. But even if Israel had accepted Jesus, animal sacrifice would have ended, nonetheless. Because as the true Lamb of God Jesus would have died for the redemption of Israel and the world just the same—that singular event permanently ended animal sacrifice. There is no continuing need for it in the economy of God.

In other words, if Israel had accepted Jesus as their Messiah at His first Advent, He would have still died for the redemption for humankind anyway, and the Old Testament worship system would have still come to an end. Jesus Christ would have still fulfilled the Hebrew Scriptures perfectly. God's purpose could not be aborted in anyway (Isa. 55:10-11).

Furthermore, the New Covenant worship system would have been implemented just the same with Israel in charge. Jesus building the Church would not have been necessary, because Israel would have done what the Church now does.

Israel would evangelize the world, bringing salvation to all nations (Matt.28:19-20; John 3:16). By doing this they would have fulfilled the covenant promise to Abraham that all nations on earth would be blessed through them (Gen.12:3).

Yet, there will be worship structure(s) in the millennium just as we now have small, medium, and mega church buildings. Jews and some Christians will view one such structure as the Third Temple. Jews will normally think it is a place to offer animal sacrifice; that is expected, that is the Jewish mindset.

But they are going to be surprised because the Messiah they are looking for will turn out to be the same Jesus that was crucified (Zech.12:10; John 19:33-37). That being the case, the animal sacrifice issue is resolved; there is no need for it. Jesus is not going to reinstate animal sacrifice to plicate a once backslidden worship system that failed to obey Him.

Orthodox Jews believe that when Messiah comes, they will be empowered to do evangelism work. But if the Messiah is Jesus, the Church already did that. Jesus will not be going back to the old Hebrew worship system. The book of Hebrews tells us, that old system is "obsolete," dead, faded away (Heb. 8:7-13). The old wineskin cannot contain the new wine.

Second, *the Scripture passages that speak of the building of a future temple.* We find these more extensively in Ezekiel's prophecies (40:1-46:24). Note that Ezekiel prophesied during the Babylonian captivity. His prophecy of a new temple is dated 573 B.C., before the rebuilding of the Second Temple under Zerubbabel which started 536 B.C. (see Ezra 2-4).

So, the Second Temple was in the future to Ezekiel, that includes the Herodian Temple expansion. To bypass those two massive rebuilding programs of the Jewish Temple and apply Ezekiel's temple vision to a distant, eschatological, Millennium Temple is a stretch indeed, and an unnecessary one. It is an attempt to force the Scripture to fit into some dispensational, theological scheme or framework.

Summary

There will be a Temple and you can call it third or fourth, the number is not what's important about it. Like a church building, it will be a Temple of convenience not of necessity. It will be a house of prayer and worship for all peoples, but not necessarily a sectarian, Jewish Temple such as Ezekiel speaks about.

The Third Temple will more be the center, the seat of the theocratic government of Jesus Christ. As stated earlier, His government will revolve around worship rather than the economy and money, as previous worldclass, gentile cities.

The building, though elegant, will be little more important than a church building today, in the sense that the Messiah's throne will be there. Just as the building is not the Church and will never be, neither will this massive, elegant structure.

The structure will not be an object of worship, as Jews and Samaritans made of it in first century A.D. Jesus replaced that worship system with the Church. Jesus talked about this replacement to the Samaritan woman and to His disciples (John 4:19-24; Matt.16:16-19, 24:1-2). He implemented it with the birth of the Church on the Day of Pentecost (Acts 2:1-48). And He prophesied the utter destruction of the corrupted, Jewish worship system (Matt.24:12). It was hard for the apostles to accept the end of this corrupted system (Acts 10-11, 14-15:1-35; Gal.3-5). But Jesus prophesied its demise.

Will animal sacrifice be reinstated? No! If the sum of Scripture is considered correctly, animal sacrifice will not be reinstated, despite what some scholars say. One would have to ask, reinstated to satisfy who or what? The idea that Jesus is coming back to placate a corrupted, first century worship system that He condemned is a huge mistake.

Yes, the covenant promises will be fulfilled, and Israel will play a pivotal role in the Millennium. But Jesus is not held captive to that outdated worship system. The reinstatement of animal sacrifice is nothing short of a dispensational, theological misunderstanding of Scripture.

The abundance of talk about animal sacrifice being reinstated is the old Hebraic mindset. But simply ask, for what purpose? In God's economy, animal sacrifice ended with the sacrifice of Jesus, the Lamb of God on the cross. All sacrifices of the old covenant point to Jesus and find their fulfilment in Him.

The final nail was driven in the coffin of Hebrew worship system when the Romans destroyed the Temple and Jerusalem in AD 70 as prophesied by Jesus in His Olivet discourse on the time of the end (Matt.24:1-2).

Modern Judaism without Jesus Christ is still an attempt to resuscitate that old, dead, and defunct system. Pouring new wine in old wineskin did not work then nor will it work now or at any future date. That system is not just obsolete; it is dead!

The book of Hebrews gives us the outline and facts of the New System. It includes, a new law written inwardly on human hearts, a new priesthood after the order of Melchizedek, a new spiritual sanctuary, and a new High Priest who is Jesus Himself (Heb.7-9). The new system, mediated by Jesus is far superior to the old (Heb.1-2).

The work of animal rights activists in the latter part of the Church Age will come to full fruition in the millennium because there will be greater respect for animal life. Animals will not be needed for sacrifice, and animals will not hunt each other as food anymore. The zebra can have a good night's sleep without worrying about the lions. It will be a kinder, gentler world. "The wolf will live with the lamb, the leopard will lie down with the goat, the calf and the lion and the yearling together; and a little child will lead them…" (Isa.11:6-9; 35:9, 6:5).

Finally, those who insist that Ezekiel's temple is the Third Temple of the millennial must also explain the continuation of animal sacrifice because Ezekiel's temple is designed for that purpose. That is understandable because the time of Ezekiel's writing, no Jew could conceive a Jewish temple without animal sacrifice. That was the Hebraic mindset.

But for us Christians who know that Jesus sacrifice is the end of animal sacrifice must understand the text in the light of His redemptive sacrifice on the cross. The continuation of animal sacrifice would cancel the sacrifice of Jesus or implying that it is not enough for our redemption. The case for animal sacrifice in the millennium is totally without merit.

The reinstatement of animal sacrifice in the millennium is a theological absurdity invented for a dispensational theological scheme. It is without merit and should be discarded.

Lidie H. Edmunds' classic hymn sums up the sacrificial system for us: "I need no other argument, I need no other plea, it is enough that Jesus died, and that He died for me."

CHAPTER 7
CHARACTER & DURATION OF CHRIST'S REIGN

The duration of the millennium must be distinguished from the duration of Christ's Reign. According to the biblical text, the millennium is for a thousand years (Rev.201-6). But the reign of Christ is eternal. "Of the greatness of his government and peace there will be no end. He will reign on David's throne and over his kingdom establishing and upholding it with justice and righteousness...forever"(Isa.9:7; Dan.2:44).

The preceding prophetic utterance from Isaiah speaks of the character and longevity of the Messianic kingdom and reign. The New Testament reflects the same (Heb.1:1-2: 8).

There was never a time the Son of God was not King or not reigning. He is always King and always reigning. When we say His Sonship and reign are eternal, we mean, we cannot point to a beginning in the past and we cannot point to an end in the future. His reign is eternal. To underscore the eternality of the Kingship and reign of Jesus Christ, the apostle Paul gives us the following intelligence report (Colossians 1:15-20):

> The Son is the image of the invisible God, the first firstborn over all creation. For in him all things were created: things in heaven and on earth, visible and invisible, whether thrones or powers or rulers or authorities; all things have been created through him and for him. He is before all things, and in him all things hold together. And he is the head of the body, the church; he is the beginning and the first born from among the dead, so that in everything he might have the supremacy. For God was pleased to have all his fulness dwell in him, and through him to reconcile to himself all things, whether things on earth or things heaven, by making peace through his blood shed on the cross.

The preceding quote gives us three foundational truths: 1) the Son of God has always existed with the Father and the Holy Spirit, 2) the material Universe was created through the Son, for the Son, and is held together by the Son, and 3) the redemption of humankind and the world are brought about through the Son, though not without the Father and the Holy Spirit. Given these facts and truths, therefore, we conclude that the Son has always been King and will always reign as such. But there are at least four phases to Son's eternal reign.

The Four Phases of Christ's Reign

The first is the preincarnate phase. Here, the uncreated, divine person referred to as the Word or *Logos* has always been (John 1:1, 14). As such, He is King over the Universe He created with the other two persons of the Trinity (vv.2-3).

This first phase runs from eternity to the creation of the Universe; the Universe has a beginning, but the Creator has none. The first phase continued to the time the *Logos* divested Himself of His majesty and glory to become Man (Phil.2: 5-11).

The second phase of the Son's Kingly reign began with His incarnation (John 1:14). And it will continue to His second Advent in glory. Some scholars may want to end the incarnation phase with the ascension and exaltation of Christ to the righthand of the Father, but we are keeping it as one here.

During this second phase, Christ is offered as the Lamb of God for the redemption of humankind and the world, and He initiated the establishment of the spiritual aspect of the kingdom. That is the rule of God in the hearts of humankind, often referred to as the kingdom of heaven. He also establishes the Church. During this second phase, Christ exercises the role of King/Priest (Royal-Priesthood). This role is extensively explained in the book of Hebrews as the reigning High Priest.

It is important to emphasize here that God became incarnate to establish a *Spiritual Kingdom in the hearts of humans*, not to rule on any earthly throne. The Jews and the immediate disciples of Christ had difficulty grasping this teaching at first and kept pushing Jesus to restore the Davidic

Kingdom to Israel. But Jesus wanted to rule their hearts redemptively first.

The building of the spiritual kingdom was initiated by Jesus Christ (Matt.16:16-19). He is its foundation (Eph.2:19-22). But Jesus handed-off the earthly task of kingdom building to the apostles and the blessed Holy Spirit (Acts 1:8, 2:1-47). We commonly refer to the task of kingdom building as disciple-making or evangelization of the world (Matt.28: 19-20).

You may say, God became incarnate to exercise redemptive rule over the interior kingdom of the human heart. For this reason, access to human hearts continues to be sought throughout the Church age, as the gospel is preached to the ends of the earth (Matt.28:18-20; Rom.10:9-15). This mission will end when Christ returns in glory (Matt.24:14).

The third phase of Christ's Kingship begins with His Second Advent and continues to the end of the millennium (Rev.20:1-15). During this time, we see the manifestation of the visible, earthly Kingdom. Christ returns from heaven as the warrior King (Rev.19:11-15). He puts down all opposition to His authority (vv.17-21; Isa.63:1-6). And He sits on the throne of David and reigns as KING of Kings and LORD of Lords over the whole earth (Isa.9:6-7). He remains king over the entire created order, but the emphasis is placed upon His earthy reign.

The millennial rule of the Christ demonstrates what the nations could have been if humans did not partner with Satan. The rebellion of Adam and Eve against the Creator placed the earth and humankind on a detour path from the perfect will of God. Humans went their own way like sheep gone astray (Isa.53:6). A detour is a different path to the same destination. God's plan is still realized, but for on a longer time schedule for humans; for God, that's a short time (2 Peter 3: 8-9). Israel's rejection of Jesus as the Messiah further complicated the situation; it pushes back the fulfillment of certain covenantal promises to Israel to the time of the Millennium.

The fourth phase of Christ reign as King is when he hands over the Kingdom to His Father in the new world order to eternity future. To this fourth phase, the apostle Paul gives us this intelligence report:

> Then the end will come, when he hands over the kingdom to God the Father after he has destroyed all dominion, authority, and power. For he must reign until he has put all his enemies under his feet. The last enemy to be destroyed is death….When he has done this, then the Son himself will be made subject to him who put everything under him, so that God may be all in all. (1Cor.15:24-28)

The Son handing off the kingdom to the Father, is at the end of His millennial reign, that's after the White Throne or final judgment. At that time the wicked are judged and disposed of. Satan is cast into hell, and death and hades are also cast into the lake of burning sulfur (Rev.20:11-15). All enemies and opposing authorities are dealt with by the Son of God. It is at this point the Son hands over to the kingdom to the Father and they reign together as they did before the creation of the world.

Much of the fourth phase of the Son's reign remains classified, known in full only to the blessed Holy Trinity. Perhaps, we will return to this in Volume 10. The focus of this chapter is to give more depth to the nature of the millennial reign of the Christ. We will briefly discuss five factors.

A Reign in Righteousness and Justice

Jesus will rule with a rod of iron; that is a figure of speech which means he will govern with the double strength of righteousness and justice. These are two attributes of God, righteousness, and justice. They are inherent to His essential being or nature, and that is true of all three personalities of the blessed Holy Trinity.

God created humans in His own image and likeness, and He wants them to reflect these two qualities, personally and interpersonally. But the deprave character of sin renders humans impotent living up to the divine standard without spiritual transformation (Rom.12:1-2).

For this reason, Jesus died on the cross and rose again from the dead to provide God's standard of righteousness to each person and the capabilities to live justly. Without a redemptive relationship with Jesus Christ human societies always fall short of God's ideal righteousness and justice. The millennium is the first time a perfect human being is sitting on a throne to rule over humankind. The ruler is truly God and truly Man.

The prophet Isaiah (9:6-7) speaks of this government of righteousness and justice as follows:

> For to us a child is born, to us a son is given, and the government will be on his shoulders. And he will be called Wonderful Counselor, Mighty God, Everlasting Father, Prince of Peace. Of the greatness of his government and peace there will be no end. He will reign on David's throne and over his kingdom, establishing and upholding it with justice and righteousness from that time on and forever. The zeal of the LORD Almighty will accomplish this. (Isa.9:6-7)

These preceding two verses of Scripture capture the essence and significance of Christ's government like none other. The ruling King is human because He was born as a child, and given as a son, yet he is the Mighty God, the Everlasting Father. The quote tells us where the seat of His government is located, on David's throne in Jerusalem. It tells us the nature, character, scope, and extent of His government. He rules in righteousness and justice forever. Only the Lord Almighty can pull off something this magnificent and glorious.

A Reign of Peace and Harmony

The millennial reign of the Christ upon and over the earth, is one of peace and harmony. The responsibilities of world government will be upon the shoulders of the King of Peace also known as the Prince of Peace (Isa.9:7). Nations will be at peace with each other, and their weapons of war will be transformed into agricultural equipment.

War started in heaven with a rebel angel named Lucifer. His rebellion resulted in expulsion, but he brought the same attitude and culture of war with him to earth enjoined with much anger (Rev.12:7-17). He will come to earth to expel this rogue to another place God has prepared for him.

Since Eden, he has been recruiting humans to join his cause of opposing God and His Christ. He will not stop until he is completely vanquished from the earth. Jesus calls him a liar and a thief, one who steals, kills, and destroys (Rom.10:10a).

As long as Satan is allowed to roam the earth seeking whom he may devour, humankind with not enjoy full peace God and neighbor. In His own time God will rid the creation of this rebel. For that reason, at the Second Advent of the Christ, Satan will be taken into custody and will be in prison the duration of the millennium (Rev.20:1-3). He will not be able to continue his mischief during the reign of Christ.

Since the time of Cain and Abel, human societies have been ones of war and violence. But the birth of Jesus Christ promised peace of earth and glory to God in heaven (Luke 2:8-18). Jesus lived as a man of peace, and His followers lived and promoted a nonviolent way of life. Yet, most of them died violently.

Jesus died violently to secure the peace with God and neighbor (Eph.2:11-22). But that vision of full peace on earth with neighbors has not been achieved yet. But the Prince of Peace will bring it about upon His return. His return means not just the cessation of war but the end of all wars.

A Reign of Prosperity and Flourishing

In His *First Advent* Jesus declared, "I come that they might have lift and have it more abundantly" or have it to the full (John 10:10b KJVN). But in the first half of this verse He speaks of Satan, the enemy, who comes "to steal, kill, and destroy."

The evil One from the time of Cain and Able has been cutting short human life and will continue to do so until he is taken into custody (Rev.20:1-6). And for the first time, humans will be able to experience the true fulness of life. There will be no lack for anything during the millennium. There will be no starvation on earth.

The Lord Jesus will reign of glory and majesty over the whole earth. Today in the Church age we are instructed to pray for the Kingdom of God to come that His will may be done on earth as it is in heaven. This petition in the Lord's Prayer becomes a reality when Jesus returns, put down all opposition and establishes the kingdom upon this earth. It will be a time of great joy and celebration. There will still be evil and some rebellion, but such will not be dominant on the earth anymore.

A Reign of Freedom and Joy

Humans were created for freedom and joy, qualities that come from the very Being of God. God is the very personification of freedom and Joy. In God these attributes are boundless; God shares them with His creatures, especially humans.

Humans lost their freedom and joy when they became enslaved to sin in the Paradise Garden from which they were later expelled. Humans regained paradise in Jesus Christ; the millennium is the fullest expression paradise until the new world order, when its unfolding into the future is boundless.

In other words, as much as freedom and joy have been restored in redemption, it is nothing to compare to the fullness of joy that is truly ours in Christ. Human life and the earth remain a battle ground for evil, suffering, death and dying.

The millennium is a demonstration of the fullness of freedom, Joy, prosperity, and human flourishing that awaits the people of God and the creation. When evils of all forms are eradicated from the earth, then the new world order will be in full operation with unlimited blessings.

Reign in a Near Perfect Society

In a previous chapter the disclaimer, "near perfect society" is added in front of millennium at times and I did promise to return to it and say more. Well, this is the return as promised.

From human perspectives, earth has not seen this level of perfection, peace, harmony, and human flourishing since the Fall of man and his expulsion from paradise. But from God's perspective the millennium is still not perfect because sin is still resident in human nature and that will corrupt the environment to one degree or another.

Despite Satan's imprisonment, the millennium will still have numerous sympathizers of Satan that keep his enterprise alive. Fallen humans have a sinful nature with the proclivities to serve Satan. For that reason, humans need a savior even though Satan is not personally around. Jesus remains the only Savior.

Let's look at it another way. The generations born during the millennium are not born righteous; they are sinners with a sinful nature and need a savior like any human in other periods of time. Jesus is that Savior and He is available to them, but they are free moral agents. They can choose or reject Jesus. If Jesus is rejected, Satan is the default choice.

On that basis many millennials will reject Jesus and choose Satan. For that reason, Satan is paroled from prison for a short time find supporters as numerous as the sand of the seashore. He and his followers immediately lead an assault upon Jesus Christ and His people. With that final assault the Satan's human followers are devoured by a fire from heaven and Satan himself is permanently thrown into hell (Rev.20:7-10).

The millennium ends will all opposition to God and His Christ, it is the declaration that all oppositions are put down, and permanently removed from the creation (Rev.20:11-15).

This fourth phase of the reign of the Son of God will come to an end but His eternal reign continues. In the full scheme of things Satan, evil, and human rebellion were temporary disruption in God's eternal program. Volume 8 covers the Final Judgment which is the official end of the millennial age.

REFERENCES

Introduction

1. *Merriam Webster Online Dictionary*: (https://www.merriam-webster.com/dictionary/utopia).

2. Thomas More. *Utopia* (1516). https://en.wikipedia.org/wiki/Utopia_(book).

3. Ibid.

4. John Milton. *Paradise Lost.* https://en.wikipedia.org/wiki/Paradise_Lost

5. John Milton. *Paradise Regained* (1671). https://en.wikipedia.org/wiki/Paradise_Regained.

Chapter 1

1. George Arthur Buttrick, Editor. "Millennium" in The Interpreter's Dictionary of the Bible. Vol.3. Nashville: Abingdon Press, 1962. 381

2. Benjamin Netanyahu, A Durable Peace: Israel and Its Place Among the Nations. New York: Grand Central Publishing, 1993, 2000. 9-54.

Chapter 2

1. Kenneth H. Himes. *Christianity and the Political Order: Conflict, Cooptation, and Cooperation*. Maryknoll, New York: Orbis Books, 2012. 68-71.

2. J. Dwight Pentecost. *Things To Come.* Grand Rapids, MI: Zondervan Publishing Company. 1958. 382.

3. Theodor Herzl. *A Jewish State: Proposes A Solution to the Jewish Question.* First Published in English in London 189. The special content of the Now and Then edition Published 2016.

Chapter 3

1. J. Dwight Pentecost. *Things To Come.* Grand Rapids, MI: Zondervan Publishing Company. 1958. 407-411.

2. Ibid.

Chapter 4

1. D. James Kennedy, The Real Meaning of the Zodiac. Albert Lea, MN: D. James Kennedy Ministries, 2014.

2. Carl Boberg, *How Great Thou Art.* Trans. by Stuart K. Hine https://en.wikipedia.org/wiki/How_Great_Thou_Art.

Chapter 6

1. Dr. Randall Price. "Update on The Third Temple" in *Jewish Voice.* https://www.jewishvoice.org/read/article/update-building-third-temple.

2. Ibid.
3. Ibid.

OTHER BOOKS BY THIS AUTHOR

Your Reading List for this Series (10 Volumes):

Volume 1

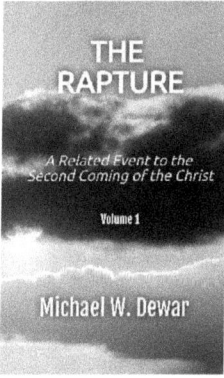

Volume 2

Volume 3

Volume 4

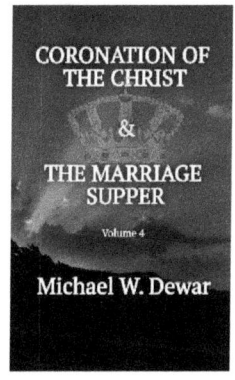

Volume 5

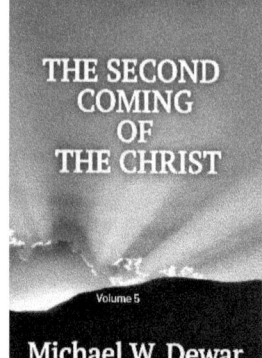

Volume 6

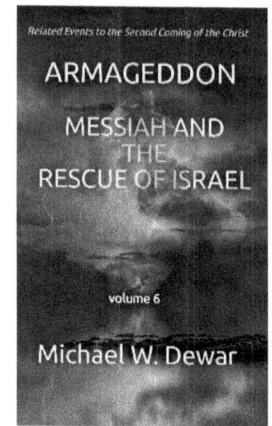

Volume 7

Volume 8

OTHER BOOKS BY THIS AUTHOR

Volume 9	Volume 10
THE FINAL JUDGMENT	THE NEW WORLD ORDER
Coming Soon	Coming Soon

*A Course of Study in Conflict Management & Resolution:
How to Launch a Peace Ministry in your Church.*

Textbook   Instructor's Manual

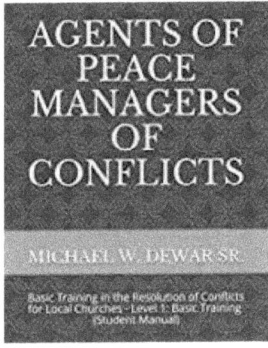

Student Manual

OTHER BOOKS BY THIS AUTHOR

The Eaten Word Package (3 products) takes you on a 40-day journey for healing, wholeness, and personal flourishing.

The Eaten Word Book comes with a Journal and a consumable known as BISCRA, each sold separately. Biscra is available on this website only (DPSCLEANSING.COM).

THE MILLENNIUM

ABOUT THE AUTHOR

Michael W. Dewar, Sr. is a pastor, Bible teacher, and mentor in the spiritual life. He is a Licensed Mater Social Worker, and a specialist in conflict management and resolution, including church and family conflicts. He trains Agents of Peace-Managers OF Conflicts to launch peace ministries in local churches.

Reverend Dewar is the founder and pastor of the New York Congregational Baptist Church (NYCBC), and the author of several books, including a tree-volume training course on *Church and Family Conflicts.*

He holds earned degrees from several institutions of higher learning, including the Master of Divinity from what is now Palmer Theological Seminary, Eastern University, the Master of Social Work from Wurzweiler School of Social Work, Yeshiva University, the LMSW from the State of New York, and a doctorate from Regent University, School of Divinity.

At the time of this publication, Reverend Dewar pastors in New York where he lives with his family.

THE MILLENNIUM

ABOUT THE AUTHOR

THE MILLENNIUM

www.ingramcontent.com/pod-product-compliance
Lightning Source LLC
Chambersburg PA
CBHW071716040426
42446CB00011B/2095